KU-253-096

easy

Soups

easy
Soups

MARKS &
SPENCER

Marks and Spencer p.l.c.
PO Box 3339
Chester CH99 9QS

shop online
www.marksandspencer.com

Copyright © Exclusive Editions 2007

Photography by Clive Bozzard Hill and Mike Cooper
Food Styling by Carol Tennent, Val Barrett, Carol Handslip and Sumi Glass
Introduction by Anne Sheasby

All rights reserved. No part of this publication may be reproduced, stored in a retrieval system or transmitted, in any form or by any means, electronic, mechanical, photocopying, recording or otherwise, without the prior permission of the copyright holder.

ISBN: 978-1-84461-985-6

Printed in China

The views expressed in this book are those of the author but they are general views only and readers are urged to consult a relevant and qualified specialist for individual advice in particular situations. Marks and Spencer p.l.c. and Exclusive Editions hereby exclude all liability to the extent permitted by law for any errors or omissions in this book and for any loss, damage or expense (whether direct or indirect) suffered by a third party relying on any information contained in this book.

NOTES FOR THE READER
This book uses both metric and imperial measurements. Follow the same units of measurement throughout; do not mix metric and imperial. All spoon measurements are level unless otherwise stated: teaspoons are assumed to be 5ml and tablespoons are assumed to be 15ml. Unless otherwise stated, milk is assumed to be semi-skimmed, eggs and individual vegetables such as potatoes are medium, and pepper is freshly ground black pepper. Sufferers from liver disease and those with weakened immune systems should never eat raw fish. Recipes using raw or very lightly cooked eggs should be avoided by infants, the elderly, pregnant women, convalescents and anyone suffering from an illness. The times given are an approximate guide only. Preparation times differ according to the techniques used by different people and the cooking times may also vary from those given. Optional ingredients, variations or serving suggestions have not been included in the calculations.

FSC

Mixed Sources
Product group from well-managed forests and other controlled sources
www.fsc.org Cert no.SGS-COC-003450
© 1996 Forest Stewardship Council

Contents

	Introduction	6
1	Vegetarian	10
2	Fish & Shellfish	46
3	Meat	84
4	Chicken & Poultry	122
	Index	160

Introduction

Soups are appealing in so many ways because they are versatile, easy to prepare and are full of flavour and goodness, making them a nutritious and satisfying choice. Soups can be served as a starter, a light meal or as a snack, and the more substantial hearty soups can be served as a meal in themselves.

Rich and warming soups are ideal for chilly autumnal or wintry days, chilled soups are perfect for summer dining al fresco, wholesome soups are a good choice for a filling lunch or supper, and light, delicate soups provide an appetizing starter for a dinner party or family celebration.

Homemade Soups

Soups can be made using many different ingredients and are perfect for making the most of seasonal ingredients. Typically, most soups are savoury, but some (often sweet) fruit-based soups are also popular in some countries. When making soup, using a good-quality, well-flavoured stock is key to creating a really delicious soup.

Good, home-made stocks are preferable, but if you are short of time, choose from an improved range of stock products available on the market, including chilled fresh stock, bouillon powder or concentrated liquid stock.

Alternatively, save the cooking water when boiling or steaming vegetables, and add it to soups instead of some or all of the stock, for extra flavour.

Some soups are served chunky-style, while many are served all or partly-puréed, so when making soup at home, a blender, liquidizer or food processor (or a hand-held/stick blender) will prove to be a real bonus. A large, preferably heavy-based, saucepan is also ideal for cooking soup.

Small dumplings and small pasta (known as pastina or 'soup pasta') add substance to some soups, and ground almonds or oatmeal can be stirred into soup to thicken, enrich and add flavour and texture.

Many soups freeze well, providing an ideal stand-by for when you have less time to prepare and cook a meal. Single servings of soup can also be frozen in small individual containers for convenience. Simply remove the soup from the freezer and defrost it, then reheat it gently, but thoroughly, until hot.

Croûtons & Other Accompaniments

Plenty of fresh crusty bread or bread rolls, served warm or cold, is often the only accompaniment a soup needs, but alternative choices such as croûtons, melba toast, bruschetta and garlic bread will equally enhance even the simplest of soups.

Croûtons (small cubes of crisp, golden fried bread) add a lovely finishing touch to a wide variety of puréed soups, adding extra flavour, crunch and appeal. Croûtons can be made from many types of plain bread, including white, wholemeal or granary, as well as from flavoured breads such as sun-dried tomato, olive, herb or cheese breads.

Bread slices can also be cut into different mini shapes rather than small squares to make the croûtons more attractive. Try tossing the hot croûtons in chopped fresh herbs or freshly grated Parmesan, or sprinkle them with ground spices to add extra flavour and appeal.

Garnishing Soup

Garnishes provide the decorative finishing touch to many soups and they should look attractive and complement the flavours of the soup. A sprinkling of chopped fresh parsley or snipped fresh chives may be all that is required. A swirl or two of cream, crème fraiche or plain yogurt in the centre of each serving looks lovely, especially if it is then feathered with a cocktail stick or skewer. Top with a scattering of finely chopped spring onion, crispy bacon bits or a sprinkling of paprika, chilli powder or black pepper to add the finishing touch.

Small sprigs of fresh herbs such as thyme, basil, rosemary or watercress sprigs also look great. A light sprinkling of finely grated or thinly shaved hard cheese such as fresh Parmesan or Cheddar, or a little crumbled blue cheese, adds extra delicious flavour to many soups.

For a slightly more elaborate garnish, top each portion with a spoonful of pesto or herb pistou (similar to pesto) – ideal for tomato or vegetable soups – and swirl it in just before serving. A drizzle of olive, chilli or sesame oil works really well as a garnish on some soups and thinly pared fruit zests such as shreds of orange or lemon suit other soups.

Vegetable Stock

Makes: about 2 litres/3½ pints

Ingredients

2 tbsp sunflower oil
115 g/4 oz onion, finely chopped
40 g/1½ oz leek, finely chopped
115 g/4 oz carrots, finely chopped
4 celery sticks, finely chopped
85 g/3 oz fennel, finely chopped
1 small tomato, finely chopped
2.25 litres/4 pints water
1 bouquet garni

Heat the oil in a large saucepan. Add the onion and leek and cook over a low heat, stirring occasionally, for 5 minutes, until softened. Add the remaining vegetables, cover and cook for 10 minutes. Add the water and bouquet garni, bring to the boil and simmer for 20 minutes.

Strain the stock into a bowl, leave to cool, cover and store in the refrigerator. Use immediately or freeze in portions for up to 3 months.

Fish Stock

Makes: about 1.3 litres/2¼ pints

Ingredients

650 g/1 lb 7 oz white fish heads, bones and trimmings, rinsed
1 onion, sliced
2 celery sticks, chopped
1 carrot, sliced
1 bay leaf
4 fresh parsley sprigs
4 black peppercorns
½ lemon, sliced
1.3 litres/2¼ pints water
125 ml/4 fl oz dry white wine

Cut out and discard the gills from any fish heads, then place the heads, bones and trimmings in a saucepan. Add all the remaining ingredients and gradually bring to the boil, skimming off the scum that rises to the surface. Partially cover and simmer for 25 minutes.

Strain the stock without pressing down on the contents of the sieve. Leave to cool, cover and store in the refrigerator. Use immediately or freeze in portions for up to 3 months.

Chicken Stock

Makes: about 2.5 litres/4½ pints

Ingredients

1.3 kg/3 lb chicken wings and necks

2 onions, cut into wedges

4 litres/7 pints water

2 carrots, coarsely chopped

2 celery sticks, coarsely chopped

10 fresh parsley sprigs

4 fresh thyme sprigs

2 bay leaves

10 black peppercorns

Put the chicken wings and necks and the onions in a large saucepan and cook over a low heat, stirring frequently, until lightly browned.

Add the water and stir well to scrape off any sediment from the base of the pan. Gradually bring to the boil, skimming off the scum that rises to the surface. Add all the remaining ingredients, partially cover and simmer for 3 hours.

Strain the stock into a bowl, leave to cool, cover and store in the refrigerator. When cold, remove and discard the layer of fat from the surface. Use immediately or freeze in portions for up to 6 months.

Beef Stock

Makes: about 1.7 litres/3 pints

Ingredients

1 kg/2 lb 4 oz beef marrow bones,
    sawn into 7.5-cm/3-inch pieces

650 g/1 lb 7 oz stewing steak in a single piece

2.8 litres/5 pints water

4 cloves

2 onions, halved

2 celery sticks, coarsely chopped

8 black peppercorns

1 bouquet garni

Place the bones in the base of a large saucepan and put the meat on top. Add the water and gradually bring to the boil, skimming off the scum that rises to the surface.

Press a clove into each onion half and add to the pan with the celery, peppercorns and bouquet garni. Partially cover and simmer for 3 hours. Remove the meat and simmer for 1 hour more.

Strain the stock into a bowl, leave to cool, cover and store in the refrigerator. When cold, remove and discard the layer of fat from the surface. Use immediately or freeze in portions for up to 6 months.

Vegetarian

Tomato Soup

serves 4

55 g/2 oz butter

1 small onion, finely chopped

450 g/1 lb tomatoes, coarsely chopped

1 bay leaf

3 tbsp plain flour

600 ml/1 pint milk

salt and pepper

sprigs of fresh basil, to garnish

Melt half the butter in a saucepan. Add the onion and cook over a low heat, stirring occasionally, for 5–6 minutes until softened. Add the tomatoes and bay leaf and cook, stirring occasionally, for 15 minutes, or until pulpy.

Meanwhile, melt the remaining butter in another saucepan. Add the flour and cook, stirring constantly, for 1 minute. Remove the pan from the heat and gradually stir in the milk. Return to the heat, season with salt and pepper and bring to the boil, stirring constantly. Continue to cook, stirring, until smooth and thickened.

When the tomatoes are pulpy, remove the pan from the heat. Discard the bay leaf and pour the tomato mixture into a blender or food processor. Process until smooth, then push through a sieve into a clean saucepan. Bring the tomato mixture to the boil, then gradually stir it into the milk mixture. Season to taste with salt and pepper. Ladle into warmed bowls, garnish with basil and serve immediately.

Leek & Potato Soup

serves 4–6

55 g/2 oz butter

1 onion, chopped

3 leeks, sliced

225 g/8 oz potatoes, cut into 2-cm/¾-inch cubes

850 ml/1½ pints vegetable stock

salt and pepper

150 ml/5 fl oz single cream, to serve (optional)

2 tbsp snipped fresh chives, to garnish

Melt the butter in a large saucepan over a medium heat, add the onion, leeks and potatoes and sauté gently for 2–3 minutes, until soft but not brown. Pour in the stock, bring to the boil, then reduce the heat and simmer, covered, for 15 minutes.

Transfer the mixture to a food processor or blender and process until smooth. Return to the rinsed-out saucepan.

Heat the soup, season with salt and pepper to taste and serve in warmed bowls, swirled with the cream, if using, and garnished with chives.

Chunky Vegetable Soup

serves 6

2 carrots, sliced

1 onion, diced

1 garlic clove, crushed

350 g/12 oz new potatoes, diced

2 celery sticks, sliced

115 g/4 oz closed-cup mushrooms, quartered

400 g/14 oz canned chopped tomatoes

600 ml/1 pint vegetable stock

1 bay leaf

1 tsp dried mixed herbs or 1 tbsp chopped fresh mixed herbs

85 g/3 oz sweetcorn kernels, frozen or canned, drained

55 g/2 oz green cabbage, shredded

freshly ground black pepper

sprigs of fresh basil, to garnish (optional)

Put the carrots, onion, garlic, potatoes, celery, mushrooms, tomatoes and stock into a large saucepan. Stir in the bay leaf and herbs. Bring to the boil, then reduce the heat, cover and simmer for 25 minutes.

Add the sweetcorn and cabbage and return to the boil. Reduce the heat, cover and simmer for 5 minutes, or until the vegetables are tender. Remove and discard the bay leaf. Season to taste with pepper.

Ladle into warmed bowls, garnish with basil, if using, and serve immediately.

Minestrone

serves 4

2 tbsp olive oil

2 garlic cloves, chopped

2 red onions, chopped

1 red pepper, deseeded and chopped

1 orange pepper, deseeded and chopped

400 g/14 oz canned chopped tomatoes

1 litre/1¾ pints vegetable stock

1 celery stick, chopped

400 g/14 oz canned borlotti beans

100 g/3½ oz green leafy cabbage, shredded

75 g/2¾ oz frozen peas, defrosted

1 tbsp chopped fresh parsley

75 g/2¾ oz dried vermicelli

salt and pepper

freshly grated Parmesan cheese, to garnish

Heat the oil in a large saucepan over a medium heat, add the garlic and onions and cook, stirring, for 3 minutes, until slightly softened. Add the red and orange peppers and the chopped tomatoes and cook for a further 2 minutes, stirring. Stir in the stock, then add the celery. Drain and add the borlotti beans along with the cabbage, peas and parsley. Season with salt and pepper. Bring to the boil, then lower the heat and simmer for 30 minutes.

Add the vermicelli to the pan. Cook for a further 10–12 minutes, or according to the instructions on the packet. Remove from the heat and ladle into serving bowls. Garnish with freshly grated Parmesan and serve immediately.

Red Pepper & Orange Soup

serves 4

5 blood oranges

3 tbsp olive oil

1.5 kg/3 lb 5 oz red peppers, deseeded and sliced

1½ tbsp orange flower water

salt and pepper

extra virgin olive oil, for drizzling (optional)

Finely grate the rind of one of the oranges and shred the rind of another with a citrus zester. Set aside. Squeeze the juice from all the oranges.

Heat the oil in a saucepan, add the red peppers and cook over a medium heat, stirring occasionally, for 10 minutes. Stir in the grated orange rind and cook for a further few minutes. Reduce the heat, cover and simmer gently, stirring occasionally, for 20 minutes.

Remove the pan from the heat, leave to cool slightly, then transfer the red pepper mixture to a food processor and process to a smooth purée. Add the orange juice and orange flower water and process again until thoroughly combined.

Transfer the soup to a bowl, season to taste with salt and leave to cool completely, then cover with clingfilm and chill in the refrigerator for 3 hours. Stir well before serving sprinkled with the shredded orange rind and drizzled with extra virgin olive oil, if using.

French Onion Soup

serves 6

3 tbsp olive oil

675 g/1 lb 8 oz onions, thinly sliced

4 garlic cloves, 3 chopped and 1 halved

1 tsp sugar

2 tsp chopped fresh thyme, plus extra sprigs to garnish

2 tbsp plain flour

125 ml/4 fl oz dry white wine

2 litres/3½ pints vegetable stock

6 slices French bread

300 g/10½ oz Gruyère cheese, grated

Heat the oil in a large, heavy-based saucepan over a medium-low heat, add the onions and cook, stirring occasionally, for 10 minutes, or until they are just beginning to brown. Stir in the chopped garlic, sugar and chopped thyme, then reduce the heat and cook, stirring occasionally, for 30 minutes, or until the onions are golden brown.

Sprinkle in the flour and cook, stirring constantly, for 1–2 minutes. Stir in the wine. Gradually stir in the stock and bring to the boil, skimming off any scum that rises to the surface, then reduce the heat and simmer for 45 minutes.

Meanwhile, preheat the grill to medium. Toast the bread on both sides under the grill, then rub the toast with the cut edges of the halved garlic clove.

Ladle the soup into 6 flameproof bowls set on a baking tray. Float a piece of toast in each bowl and divide the grated cheese between them. Place under the grill for 2–3 minutes, or until the cheese has just melted. Garnish with thyme sprigs and serve at once.

Cream of Pea Soup

serves 4

115 g/4 oz butter

1 onion, finely chopped

450 g/1 lb shelled peas

150 ml/5 fl oz water

600–700 ml/1–1¼ pints milk

salt and pepper

Melt the butter in a saucepan over a low heat. Add the onion and cook, stirring occasionally, for 5 minutes until softened.

Add the peas and pour in the water. Increase the heat to medium and simmer for 3–4 minutes, or until the peas are tender. (Frozen peas will be ready in 10 minutes.)

Add 600 ml/1 pint of the milk, season with salt and pepper and then bring to the boil, stirring constantly.

Remove the pan from the heat and leave to cool slightly, then pour the soup into a food processor and process to a smooth purée.

Return the soup to the rinsed-out pan and bring back to the boil. If the soup seems too thick, heat the remaining milk in a small saucepan and stir it into the soup. Taste and adjust the seasoning if necessary, and serve.

Gazpacho

serves 4

250 g/9 oz white bread slices, crusts removed

700 g/1 lb 9 oz tomatoes, peeled and chopped

3 garlic cloves, coarsely chopped

2 red peppers, deseeded and coarsely chopped

1 cucumber, peeled, deseeded and chopped

5 tbsp extra virgin olive oil

5 tbsp red wine vinegar

1 tbsp tomato purée

850 ml/1½ pints water

salt and pepper

4 ice cubes, to serve

Tear the bread into pieces and place in a food processor or blender. Process briefly to make breadcrumbs and transfer to a large bowl. Add the tomatoes, garlic, red peppers, cucumber, oil, vinegar and tomato purée. Mix well.

Working in batches, place the tomato mixture with about the same amount of the measured water in the food processor or blender and process to a purée. Transfer to another bowl. When all the tomato mixture and water have been blended together, stir well and season to taste with salt and pepper. Cover with clingfilm and chill in the refrigerator for at least 2 hours, but no longer than 12 hours.

When ready to serve, pour the soup into chilled serving bowls and float an ice cube in each bowl.

Creamy Mushroom & Tarragon Soup

serves 4–6

50 g/1¾ oz butter

1 onion, chopped

700 g/1 lb 9 oz button mushrooms, coarsely chopped

850 ml/1½ pints vegetable stock

3 tbsp chopped fresh tarragon, plus extra to garnish

150 ml/5 fl oz crème fraîche

salt and pepper

Melt half the butter in a large saucepan. Add the onion and cook gently for 10 minutes, until soft. Add the remaining butter and the mushrooms and cook for 5 minutes, or until the mushrooms are browned.

Stir in the stock and tarragon, bring to the boil, then reduce the heat and leave to simmer gently for 20 minutes. Transfer to a food processor or blender and process until smooth. Return the soup to the rinsed-out saucepan.

Stir in the crème fraîche and add salt and pepper to taste. Reheat the soup gently until hot. Ladle into warmed serving bowls and garnish with chopped tarragon. Serve immediately.

Vegetable Soup with Pesto

serves 6

1 tbsp olive oil

1 onion, finely chopped

1 large leek, thinly sliced

1 celery stick, thinly sliced

1 carrot, quartered and thinly sliced

1 garlic clove, finely chopped

1.4 litres/2½ pints water

1 potato, diced

1 parsnip, finely diced

1 small kohlrabi or turnip, diced

150 g/5½ oz French beans, cut in small pieces

150 g/5½ oz fresh or frozen peas

2 small courgettes, quartered lengthways and sliced

400 g/14 oz canned flageolet beans, drained and rinsed

100 g/3½ oz spinach leaves, cut into thin ribbons

salt and pepper

shop-bought jar of basil pesto

Heat the olive oil in a large saucepan over a medium-low heat. Add the onion and leek and cook for 5 minutes, stirring occasionally, until the onion softens. Add the celery, carrot and garlic and cook, covered, for a further 5 minutes, stirring frequently.

Add the water, potato, parsnip, kohlrabi and French beans. Bring to the boil, reduce the heat to low and simmer, covered, for 5 minutes.

Add the peas, courgettes and flageolet beans, and season generously with salt and pepper. Cover again and simmer for about 25 minutes until all the vegetables are tender.

Add the spinach to the soup and simmer for a further 5 minutes. Taste and adjust the seasoning and stir about a tablespoon of the pesto into the soup. Ladle into warmed bowls and serve with any remaining pesto.

Tuscan Bean Soup

serves 6

300 g/10½ oz canned cannellini beans, drained and rinsed

300 g/10½ oz canned borlotti beans, drained and rinsed

600 ml/1 pint chicken or vegetable stock

115 g/4 oz dried conchigliette or other small pasta shapes

4 tbsp olive oil

2 garlic cloves, very finely chopped

3 tbsp chopped fresh flat-leaf parsley

salt and pepper

Place half the cannellini and half the borlotti beans in a food processor with half the chicken stock and process until smooth. Pour into a large, heavy-based saucepan and add the remaining beans. Stir in enough of the remaining stock to achieve the consistency you like, then bring to the boil.

Add the pasta and return to the boil, then reduce the heat and cook for 15 minutes, or until just tender.

Meanwhile, heat 3 tablespoons of the oil in a small frying pan. Add the garlic and cook, stirring constantly, for 2–3 minutes, or until golden. Stir the garlic into the soup with the parsley.

Season to taste with salt and pepper and ladle into warmed soup bowls. Drizzle with the remaining olive oil to taste and serve immediately.

Creamy Carrot & Parsnip Soup

serves 4

4 tbsp butter

1 large onion, chopped

450 g/1 lb carrots, chopped

2 large parsnips, chopped

1 tbsp grated fresh root ginger

1 tsp grated orange rind

600 ml/1 pint vegetable stock

125 ml/4 fl oz single cream

salt and pepper

sprigs of fresh coriander, to garnish

Melt the butter in a large saucepan over a low heat. Add the onion and cook, stirring, for 3 minutes, until slightly softened. Add the carrots and parsnips, cover the pan and cook, stirring occasionally, for about 15 minutes, until the vegetables have softened a little. Stir in the ginger, orange rind and stock. Bring to the boil, then reduce the heat, cover the pan and simmer for 30–35 minutes, until the vegetables are tender. Remove from the heat and leave to cool for 10 minutes.

Transfer the soup to a food processor or blender and process until smooth. Return the soup to the rinsed-out saucepan, stir in the cream and season well with salt and pepper. Warm through gently over a low heat.

Remove from the heat and ladle into soup bowls. Garnish each bowl with pepper and a sprig of coriander and serve.

Watercress Soup

serves 4

2 bunches of watercress (about 200 g/7 oz), thoroughly cleaned

40 g/1½ oz butter

2 onions, chopped

225 g/8 oz potatoes, coarsely chopped

1.2 litres/2 pints vegetable stock or water

whole nutmeg, for grating (optional)

salt and pepper

125 ml/4 fl oz crème fraîche, to serve

Remove the leaves from the stalks of the watercress and set aside. Roughly chop the stalks.

Melt the butter in a large saucepan over a medium heat, add the onions and cook for 4–5 minutes, until soft. Do not brown.

Add the potatoes to the saucepan and mix well with the onions. Add the watercress stalks and the stock.

Bring to the boil, then reduce the heat, cover and simmer for 15–20 minutes, until the potato is soft.

Add the watercress leaves and stir in to heat through. Remove from the heat and transfer to a food processor or blender. Process until smooth and return the soup to the rinsed-out saucepan. Reheat and season with salt and pepper to taste, adding a good grating of nutmeg if using.

Serve in warmed bowls with the crème fraîche spooned on top and an extra grating of nutmeg, if desired.

Spiced Pumpkin Soup

serves 4

2 tbsp olive oil

1 onion, chopped

1 garlic clove, chopped

1 tbsp chopped fresh root ginger

1 small red chilli, deseeded and finely chopped

2 tbsp chopped fresh coriander

1 bay leaf

1 kg/2 lb 4 oz pumpkin, peeled, deseeded and diced

600 ml/1 pint vegetable stock

salt and pepper

single cream, to garnish

Heat the oil in a saucepan over a medium heat. Add the onion and garlic and cook, stirring, for about 4 minutes, until slightly softened. Add the ginger, chilli, coriander, bay leaf and pumpkin and cook for another 3 minutes.

Pour in the stock and bring to the boil. Using a slotted spoon, skim any scum from the surface. Reduce the heat and simmer gently, stirring occasionally, for about 25 minutes, or until the pumpkin is tender. Remove from the heat, take out the bay leaf and leave to cool a little.

Transfer the soup to a food processor or blender and process until smooth (you may have to do this in batches). Return the mixture to the rinsed-out pan and season to taste with salt and pepper. Reheat gently, stirring. Remove from the heat, pour into 4 warmed soup bowls, garnish each one with a swirl of cream and serve.

Roasted Squash, Sweet Potato & Garlic Soup

serves 6–8

1 sweet potato, about 350 g/12 oz

1 acorn squash

4 shallots

2 tbsp olive oil

5–6 garlic cloves, unpeeled

850 ml/1½ pints chicken stock

125 ml/4 fl oz single cream

salt and pepper

snipped chives, to garnish

Preheat the oven to 190°C/375°F/Gas Mark 5.

Cut the sweet potato, squash and shallots in half lengthways, through to the stem end. Scoop the seeds out of the squash. Brush the cut sides with the oil.

Put the vegetables, cut-side down, in a shallow roasting tin. Add the garlic cloves. Roast in the preheated oven for about 40 minutes, until tender and light brown.

When cool, scoop the flesh from the potato and squash halves and put in a saucepan with the shallots. Remove the garlic peel and add the soft insides to the other vegetables.

Add the stock and a pinch of salt. Bring just to the boil, reduce the heat and simmer, partially covered, for about 30 minutes, stirring occasionally, until the vegetables are very tender.

Allow the soup to cool, then transfer to a food processor or blender and process until smooth, working in batches if necessary.

Return the soup to the saucepan and stir in the cream. Season with salt and pepper, and then reheat. Ladle into warmed bowls, garnish with snipped chives and serve.

Spinach & Cheese Soup

serves 6–8

225 g/8 oz fresh baby spinach leaves, tough stalks removed

600 ml/1 pint milk

700 ml/1¼ pints vegetable or chicken stock

200 g/7 oz Boursin or other cream cheese flavoured with garlic and herbs

salt and pepper

croûtons (optional)

Put the spinach in a large saucepan and pour in the milk and stock. Bring to the boil, then reduce the heat and simmer gently for 12 minutes. Remove the pan from the heat and leave to cool completely.

Ladle the cold soup into a food processor, in batches if necessary, and process until smooth. Cut the cheese into chunks and add to the soup. Process again until smooth and creamy.

Pour the soup into a bowl and season to taste with salt and pepper. Cover with clingfilm and leave to chill in the refrigerator for at least 3 hours. Stir well before ladling into bowls. Add croûtons, if using, and serve immediately.

Sweet potato & Stilton Soup

serves 4

4 tbsp butter

1 large onion, chopped

2 leeks, trimmed and sliced

175 g/6 oz sweet potatoes, peeled and diced

850 ml/1½ pints vegetable stock

1 tbsp chopped fresh parsley

1 bay leaf

150 ml/5 fl oz double cream

150 g/5½ oz Stilton cheese, crumbled

2 tbsp finely crumbled Stilton cheese, to garnish

pepper

slices of fresh bread, to serve

Melt the butter in a large saucepan over a medium heat. Add the onion and leeks and cook, stirring, for about 3 minutes, until slightly softened. Add the sweet potatoes and cook for a further 5 minutes, stirring, then pour in the stock, add the parsley and bay leaf and season with pepper. Bring to the boil, then lower the heat, cover the pan and simmer for about 30 minutes. Remove from the heat and leave to cool for 10 minutes. Remove the bay leaf.

Transfer half of the soup into a food processor and blend until smooth. Return to the pan with the rest of the soup, stir in the cream and cook for a further 5 minutes. Gradually stir in the crumbled Stilton until melted (do not let the soup boil).

Remove from the heat and ladle into serving bowls. Garnish with finely crumbled Stilton and serve with slices of fresh bread.

Fish &
Shellfish

Bouillabaisse

serves 4

100 ml/3½ fl oz olive oil

3 garlic cloves, chopped

2 onions, chopped

2 tomatoes, deseeded and chopped

700 ml/1¼ pints fish stock

400 ml/14 fl oz white wine

1 bay leaf

pinch of saffron threads

2 tbsp chopped fresh basil

2 tbsp chopped fresh parsley

200 g/7 oz live mussels

250 g/9 oz snapper or monkfish fillets

250 g/9 oz haddock fillets, skinned

200 g/7 oz prawns, peeled and deveined

100 g/3½ oz scallops

salt and pepper

Heat the oil in a large pan over a medium heat. Add the garlic and onions and cook, stirring, for 3 minutes. Stir in the tomatoes, stock, wine, bay leaf, saffron and herbs. Bring to the boil, reduce the heat, cover and simmer for 30 minutes.

Meanwhile, soak the mussels in lightly salted water for 10 minutes. Scrub the shells under cold running water and pull off any beards. Discard any mussels with broken shells or any that refuse to close when tapped. Put the rest into a large pan with a little water, bring to the boil and cook over a high heat for 4 minutes, or until the mussels open. Remove from the heat and discard any that remain closed.

When the tomato mixture is cooked, rinse the fish fillets, pat dry and cut into chunks. Add to the pan and simmer for 5 minutes. Add the mussels, prawns and scallops and season with salt and pepper. Cook for 3 minutes, until the fish is cooked through. Remove from the heat, discard the bay leaf and ladle into serving bowls.

Salmon & Leek Soup

serves 4

1 tbsp olive oil

1 large onion, finely chopped

3 large leeks, including green parts, thinly sliced

1 potato, finely diced

450 ml/16 fl oz fish stock

700 ml/1¼ pints water

1 bay leaf

300 g/10½ oz skinless salmon fillet, cut into 1-cm/½-inch cubes

80 ml/3 fl oz double cream

fresh lemon juice (optional)

salt and pepper

sprigs of fresh chervil or flat-leaf parsley, to garnish

Heat the oil in a heavy-based saucepan over a medium heat. Add the onion and leeks and cook for about 3 minutes until they begin to soften.

Add the potato, stock, water and bay leaf with a large pinch of salt. Bring to the boil, reduce the heat, cover and cook gently for about 25 minutes until the vegetables are tender. Remove the bay leaf.

Allow the soup to cool slightly, then transfer about half of it to a food processor or blender and process until smooth. (If using a food processor, strain off the cooking liquid and reserve. Purée half the soup solids with enough cooking liquid to moisten them, then combine with the remaining liquid.)

Return the puréed soup to the saucepan and stir to blend. Reheat gently over a medium-low heat.

Season the salmon with salt and pepper and add to the soup. Continue cooking for about 5 minutes, stirring occasionally, until the fish is tender and starts to break up. Stir in the cream, taste and adjust the seasoning, adding a little lemon juice if wished. Ladle into warmed bowls, garnish with chervil or parsley and serve.

Thai-Style Seafood Soup

serves 4

1.2 litres/2 pints fish stock

1 lemon grass stalk, split lengthways

pared rind of ½ lime, or 1 lime leaf

2.5-cm/1-inch piece fresh root ginger, sliced

¼ tsp chilli purée, or to taste

200 g/7 oz large or medium raw prawns, peeled and deveined

4–6 spring onions, sliced

250 g/9 oz scallops

2 tbsp fresh coriander leaves

salt

finely chopped red chillies, to garnish

Put the stock in a saucepan with the lemon grass, lime rind, ginger and chilli purée. Bring just to the boil, reduce the heat, cover and simmer for 10–15 minutes.

Cut the prawns almost in half lengthways, keeping the tail intact.

Strain the stock, return to the saucepan and bring to a simmer. Add the spring onions and cook for 2–3 minutes. Taste and season with salt, if needed, and stir in a little more chilli purée if wished.

Add the scallops and prawns and poach for about 1 minute until they turn opaque and the prawns curl.

Stir in the fresh coriander leaves, ladle the soup into warmed bowls, dividing the shellfish evenly, and garnish with chillies.

Prawn Laksa

serves 4

20–24 large raw unpeeled prawns

450 ml/16 fl oz fish stock

pinch of salt

1 tsp groundnut oil

450 ml/16 fl oz coconut milk

2 tsp nam pla (Thai fish sauce)

½ tbsp lime juice

115 g/4 oz dried medium rice noodles

55 g/2 oz beansprouts

sprigs of fresh coriander, to garnish

for the laksa paste

6 coriander stalks with leaves

3 large garlic cloves, crushed

1 fresh red chilli, deseeded and chopped

1 lemon grass stalk, centre part only, chopped

2.5-cm/1-inch piece fresh root ginger, peeled and chopped

1½ tbsp shrimp paste

½ tsp turmeric

2 tbsp groundnut oil

Buy unpeeled prawns, ideally with heads still intact, because you can add the shells and heads to the simmering stock to intensify the flavour.

Peel and devein the prawns, and reserve. Put the fish stock, salt and the prawn heads, peels and tails in a saucepan over a high heat and slowly bring to the boil. Lower the heat and simmer for 10 minutes.

Meanwhile, make the laksa paste. Put all the ingredients except the oil in a food processor and blend. With the motor running, slowly add up to 2 tablespoons oil just until a paste forms. (If your food processor is too large to work efficiently with this small quantity, use a pestle and mortar, or make double the quantity and keep leftovers tightly covered in the refrigerator to use another time.)

Heat the oil in a large saucepan over a high heat. Add the paste and stir-fry until it is fragrant. Strain the stock through a sieve lined with muslin. Stir the stock into the laksa paste, along with the coconut milk, nam pla and lime juice. Bring to the boil, then lower the heat, cover and simmer for 30 minutes.

Meanwhile, soak the noodles in a large bowl with enough lukewarm water to cover for 20 minutes, until soft. Alternatively, cook according to the packet instructions. Drain and set aside.

Add the prawns and beansprouts to the soup and continue simmering just until the prawns turn opaque and curl. Divide the noodles between 4 bowls and ladle the soup over, making sure everyone gets an equal share of the prawns. Garnish with the coriander and serve.

Clam & Corn Chowder

serves 4

750 g/1 lb 10 oz clams, or 280 g/10 oz canned clams

2 tbsp dry white wine (if using fresh clams)

4 tsp butter

1 large onion, finely chopped

1 small carrot, finely diced

3 tbsp plain flour

300 ml/10 fl oz fish stock

200 ml/7 fl oz water (if using canned clams)

450 g/1 lb potatoes, diced

125 g/4 oz sweetcorn, thawed if frozen

450 ml/16 fl oz full-fat milk

salt and pepper

chopped fresh flat-leaf parsley, to garnish

If using fresh clams, wash under cold running water. Discard any with broken shells or any that refuse to close when tapped. Put the clams into a heavy-based saucepan with the wine. Cover tightly, set over a medium-high heat and cook for 2–4 minutes, or until they open, shaking the pan occasionally. Discard any that remain closed. Remove the clams from the shells and strain the cooking liquid through a very fine mesh sieve; reserve both. If using canned clams, drain and rinse well.

Melt the butter in a large saucepan over a medium-low heat. Add the onion and carrot and cook for 3–4 minutes, stirring frequently, until the onion is softened. Stir in the flour and continue cooking for 2 minutes.

Slowly add about half the stock and stir well, scraping the bottom of the pan to mix in the flour. Pour in the remaining stock and the reserved clam cooking liquid, or the water if using canned clams, and bring just to the boil, stirring.

Add the potatoes, sweetcorn and milk and stir to combine. Reduce the heat and simmer gently, partially covered, for about 20 minutes, stirring occasionally, until all the vegetables are tender.

Chop the clams, if large. Stir in the clams and continue cooking for about 5 minutes until heated through. Taste and adjust the seasoning, if needed.

Ladle the soup into bowls and sprinkle with parsley.

Fennel & Tomato Soup with Prawns

serves 4

2 tsp olive oil

1 large onion, halved and sliced

2 large fennel bulbs, halved and sliced

1 small potato, diced

850 ml/1½ pints water

400 ml/14 fl oz tomato juice, plus extra if needed

1 bay leaf

125 g/4½ oz cooked peeled small prawns

2 tomatoes, skinned, deseeded and chopped

½ tsp snipped fresh dill

salt and pepper

dill sprigs or fennel fronds, to garnish

Heat the olive oil in a large saucepan over a medium heat. Add the onion and fennel and cook for 3–4 minutes, stirring occasionally, until the onion is just softened.

Add the potato, water, tomato juice and bay leaf with a large pinch of salt. Reduce the heat, cover and simmer for about 25 minutes, stirring once or twice, until the vegetables are soft.

Allow the soup to cool slightly, then transfer to a food processor or blender and process until smooth, working in batches if necessary. (If using a food processor, strain off the cooking liquid and reserve. Purée the soup solids with enough cooking liquid to moisten them, then combine with the remaining liquid.)

Return the soup to the saucepan and add the prawns. Simmer gently for about 10 minutes, to reheat the soup and allow it to absorb the prawn flavour.

Stir in the tomatoes and dill. Taste and adjust the seasoning, adding salt, if needed, and pepper. Thin the soup with a little more tomato juice, if wished. Ladle into warmed bowls, garnish with dill or fennel fronds and serve.

Genoese Fish Soup

serves 4

25 g/1 oz butter

1 onion, chopped

1 garlic clove, finely
chopped

55 g/2 oz rindless streaky
bacon, diced

2 celery sticks, chopped

400 g/14 oz canned
chopped tomatoes

150 ml/5 fl oz dry white
wine

300 ml/10 fl oz fish stock

4 fresh basil leaves, torn

2 tbsp chopped fresh
flat-leaf parsley

450 g/1 lb white fish fillets,
such as cod or monkfish,
skinned and chopped

115 g/4 oz cooked peeled
prawns

salt and pepper

Melt the butter in a large, heavy-based saucepan. Add
the onion and garlic and cook over a low heat, stirring
occasionally, for 5 minutes, or until softened.

Add the streaky bacon and celery and cook, stirring
frequently, for a further 2 minutes.

Add the tomatoes, wine, stock, basil and 1 tablespoon of
the parsley. Season to taste with salt and pepper. Bring to
the boil, then reduce the heat and simmer for 10 minutes.

Add the fish and cook for 5 minutes, or until it is opaque.
Add the prawns and heat through gently for 3 minutes.
Ladle into warmed serving bowls, garnish with the
remaining chopped parsley and serve immediately.

Cold Cucumber & Smoked Salmon Soup

serves 4

2 tsp oil

1 large onion, finely chopped

1 large cucumber, peeled, deseeded and sliced

1 small potato, diced

1 celery stick, finely chopped

1 litre/1¾ pints chicken or vegetable stock

150 ml/5 fl oz double cream

150 g/5½ oz smoked salmon, finely diced

2 tbsp snipped fresh chives

salt and pepper

Heat the oil in a large saucepan over a medium heat. Add the onion and cook for about 3 minutes, until it begins to soften.

Add the cucumber, potato, celery and stock, along with a large pinch of salt, if using unsalted stock. Bring to the boil, reduce the heat, cover and cook gently for about 20 minutes until the vegetables are tender.

Allow the soup to cool slightly, then transfer to a food processor or blender, working in batches if necessary. Purée the soup until smooth. (If using a food processor, strain off the cooking liquid and reserve it. Purée the soup solids with enough cooking liquid to moisten them, then combine with the remaining liquid.)

Transfer the puréed soup into a large container. Cover and refrigerate until cold.

Stir the cream, salmon and chives into the soup. If time permits, chill for at least 1 hour to allow the flavours to blend. Taste and adjust the seasoning, adding salt, if needed, and pepper. Ladle into chilled bowls and serve.

Seafood Chowder

serves 4

1 kg/2 lb 4 oz live mussels

4 tbsp plain flour

1.5 litres/2¾ pints fish stock

1 tbsp butter

1 large onion, finely chopped

350 g/12 oz skinless white fish fillets, such as cod, sole or haddock

200 g/7 oz cooked or raw prawns, peeled and deveined

300 ml/10 fl oz whipping cream or double cream

salt and pepper

snipped fresh dill, to garnish

Soak the mussels in lightly salted water for 10 minutes. Scrub the shells under cold running water and pull of any beards. Discard any mussels with broken shells or any that refuse to close when tapped. Put the rest in a large heavy-based saucepan with a little water, bring to the boil and cook over a high heat for 4 minutes, or until the mussels open. Remove from the heat and discard any that remain closed. When they are cool enough to handle, remove the mussels from the shells, adding any additional juices to the cooking liquid. Strain the cooking liquid through a muslin-lined sieve and reserve.

Put the flour in a mixing bowl and very slowly whisk in enough of the stock to make a thick paste. Whisk in a little more stock to make a smooth liquid.

Melt the butter in heavy-based saucepan over a medium-low heat. Add the onion, cover and cook for about 5 minutes, stirring frequently, until it softens.

Add the remaining fish stock and bring to the boil. Slowly whisk in the flour mixture until well combined and bring back to the boil, whisking constantly. Add the mussel cooking liquid. Season with salt, if needed, and pepper. Reduce the heat and simmer, partially covered, for 15 minutes.

Add the fish and mussels and continue simmering, stirring occasionally, for about 5 minutes, or until the fish is cooked and begins to flake.

Stir in the prawns and cream. Taste and adjust the seasoning. Simmer for a few minutes longer to heat through. Ladle into warmed bowls, sprinkle with dill and serve.

Seared Scallops in Garlic Broth

serves 4

1 large garlic bulb (about 100 g/3½ oz), separated into unpeeled cloves

1 celery stick, chopped

1 carrot, chopped

1 onion, chopped

10 peppercorns

5–6 parsley stems

1.2 litres/2 pints water

225 g/8 oz large sea scallops or queen scallops

1 tbsp oil

salt and pepper

fresh coriander leaves, to garnish

Combine the garlic cloves, celery, carrot, onion, peppercorns, parsley stems and water in a saucepan with a good pinch of salt. Bring to the boil, reduce the heat and simmer, partially covered, for 30–45 minutes.

Strain the stock into a clean saucepan. Taste and adjust the seasoning, and keep hot.

If using sea scallops, slice in half horizontally to form 2 thinner rounds from each. (If the scallops are very large, slice them into 3 rounds.) Sprinkle with salt and pepper.

Heat the oil in a frying pan over a medium-high heat and cook the scallops on one side for 1–2 minutes, until lightly browned and the flesh becomes opaque.

Divide the scallops between 4 warmed shallow bowls, arranging them browned-side up. Ladle the soup over the scallops, then float a few coriander leaves on top. Serve immediately.

Squid, Chorizo & Tomato Soup

serves 6

450 g/1 lb cleaned squid

150 g/5½ oz lean chorizo, peeled and very finely diced

1 onion, finely chopped

1 celery stick, thinly sliced

1 carrot, thinly sliced

2 garlic cloves, finely chopped or crushed

400 g/14 oz canned chopped tomatoes

1.2 litres/2 pints fish stock

½ tsp ground cumin

pinch of saffron

1 bay leaf

chilli purée (optional)

salt and pepper

fresh chopped flat-leaf parsley, to garnish

Cut off the squid tentacles and cut into bite-sized pieces. Slice the bodies into rings.

Place a large saucepan over a medium-low heat and add the chorizo. Cook for 5–10 minutes, stirring frequently, until it renders most of its fat. Remove with a slotted spoon and drain on paper towels.

Pour off all the fat from the pan and add the onion, celery, carrot and garlic. Cover and cook for 3–4 minutes, until the onion is slightly softened.

Stir in the tomatoes, fish stock, cumin, saffron, bay leaf and chorizo.

Add the squid to the soup. Bring almost to the boil, reduce the heat, cover and cook gently for 40–45 minutes, or until the squid and carrot are tender, stirring occasionally.

Taste the soup and stir in a little chilli purée, if using, for a spicier flavour. Season with salt and pepper. Ladle into warmed bowls, sprinkle with parsley and serve.

Lobster Bisque

serves 4

450 g/1 lb cooked lobster

45 g/1½ oz butter

1 small carrot, grated

1 celery stick, finely chopped

1 leek, finely chopped

1 small onion, finely chopped

2 shallots, finely chopped

3 tbsp brandy or Cognac

55 ml/2 fl oz dry white wine

1.2 litres/2 pints water

1 tbsp tomato purée

125 ml/4 fl oz whipping cream, or to taste

6 tbsp plain flour

2–3 tbsp water

salt and pepper

snipped fresh chives, to garnish

Pull off the lobster tail. With the legs up, cut the body in half lengthways. Scoop out the tomalley (the soft pale greenish-grey part) and, if it is a female, the roe (the solid red-orange part). Reserve these together, covered and refrigerated. Remove the meat and cut into bite-sized pieces; cover and refrigerate. Chop the shell into large pieces.

Melt half the butter in a large saucepan over a medium heat and add the lobster shell pieces. Fry until brown bits begin to stick on the bottom of the pan. Add the carrot, celery, leek, onion and shallots. Cook, stirring, for 1½–2 minutes (do not allow to burn). Add the brandy and wine and bubble for 1 minute. Pour over the water, add the tomato purée, a large pinch of salt and bring to the boil. Reduce the heat, simmer for 30 minutes and strain the stock, discarding the solids.

Melt the remaining butter in a small saucepan and add the tomalley and roe, if any. Add the cream, whisk to mix well, remove from the heat and set aside.

Put the flour in a small mixing bowl and very slowly whisk in the cold water. Stir in a little of the hot stock mixture to make a smooth liquid.

Bring the remaining lobster stock to the boil and whisk in the flour mixture. Boil gently for 4–5 minutes, or until the soup thickens. Press the tomalley, roe and cream mixture through a sieve into the soup. Simmer until heated through.

Taste and adjust the seasoning, adding more cream if wished. Ladle into bowls, sprinkle with chives and serve.

Tuna Chowder

serves 4

2 tbsp butter

1 large garlic clove, chopped

1 large onion, sliced

1 carrot, peeled and chopped

600 ml/1 pint fish stock

400 g/14 oz potatoes, peeled and cut into bite-sized chunks

400 g/14 oz canned chopped tomatoes

400 g/14 oz canned cannellini beans, drained

1 tbsp tomato purée

salt and pepper

1 courgette, trimmed and chopped

225 g/8 oz canned tuna in brine, drained

1 tbsp chopped fresh basil

1 tbsp chopped fresh parsley

100 ml/3½ fl oz double cream

sprigs of fresh basil, to garnish

Melt the butter in a large saucepan over a low heat. Add the garlic and onion and cook, stirring, for 3 minutes, until slightly softened. Add the carrot and cook for a further 5 minutes, stirring. Pour in the stock, then add the potatoes, tomatoes, beans and tomato purée. Season with salt and pepper. Bring to the boil, then reduce the heat, cover the pan and simmer for 20 minutes.

Add the courgette, tuna, and chopped basil and parsley and cook for a further 15 minutes. Stir in the cream and cook very gently for a further 2 minutes.

Remove from the heat and ladle into individual serving bowls. Garnish with sprigs of fresh basil, and serve.

Creamy Oyster Soup

serves 4

12 oysters

2 tbsp butter

2 shallots, finely chopped

5 tbsp white wine

300 ml/10 fl oz fish stock

175 ml/6 fl oz whipping or double cream

2 tbsp cornflour, dissolved in 2 tbsp cold water

salt and pepper

caviar or lumpfish roe, to garnish (optional)

To open the oysters, hold flat-side up, over a sieve set over a bowl to catch the juices, and push an oyster knife into the hinge. Work it around until you can prise off the top shell. When all the oysters have been opened, strain the liquid through a sieve lined with damp muslin. Remove any bits of shell stuck to the oysters and reserve them in their liquid.

Melt half the butter in a saucepan over a low heat. Add the shallots and cook gently for about 5 minutes, until just softened, stirring frequently; do not allow them to brown.

Add the wine, bring to the boil and boil for 1 minute. Stir in the fish stock, bring back to the boil and boil for 3–4 minutes. Reduce the heat to a gentle simmer.

Add the oysters and their liquid and poach for about 1 minute, until they become more firm but are still tender. Remove the oysters with a slotted spoon and reserve, covered. Strain the stock.

Bring the strained stock to the boil in a clean saucepan. Add the cream and bring back to the boil.

Stir the dissolved cornflour into the soup and boil gently for 2–3 minutes, stirring frequently, until slightly thickened. Add the oysters and cook for 1–2 minutes to reheat them. Taste and adjust the seasoning, if necessary, and ladle the soup into warmed bowls. Top each serving with a teaspoon of caviar or roe, if using.

Mixed Fish Soup

serves 4

1 tbsp butter

2 shallots, chopped

1 leek, trimmed and sliced

3 tbsp plain flour

500 ml/18 fl oz fish stock

1 bay leaf

500 ml/18 fl oz milk

2 tbsp dry sherry

2 tbsp lemon juice

300 g/10½ oz haddock fillets, skinned

300 g/10½ oz cod fillets, skinned

200 g/7 oz canned or freshly cooked crabmeat

150 g/5½ oz canned sweetcorn, drained

200 ml/7 fl oz double cream

salt and pepper

sprigs of fresh dill and wedges of lemon, to garnish

Melt the butter in a large saucepan over a medium heat. Add the shallots and leek and cook, stirring, for about 3 minutes, until slightly softened. In a bowl, mix the flour with enough stock to make a smooth paste, then stir it into the pan. Cook, stirring, for 2 minutes, then gradually stir in the remaining stock. Add the bay leaf and season with salt and pepper. Bring to the boil, then lower the heat. Pour in the milk and sherry, and stir in the lemon juice. Simmer for 15 minutes.

Rinse the haddock and cod fillets under cold running water, then drain and cut into bite-sized chunks. Add to the soup with the crabmeat and sweetcorn. Cook for 15 minutes, until the fish is tender and cooked through. Stir in the cream. Cook for another 2–3 minutes, then remove from the heat and discard the bay leaf.

Ladle into serving bowls, garnish with sprigs of fresh dill and lemon wedges and serve.

Crab & Vegetable Soup

serves 4

2 tbsp chilli oil

1 garlic clove, chopped

4 spring onions, trimmed and sliced

2 red peppers, deseeded and chopped

1 tbsp grated fresh root ginger

1 litre/1¾ pints fish stock

100 ml/3½ fl oz coconut milk

100 ml/3½ fl oz rice wine or sherry

2 tbsp lime juice

1 tbsp grated lime rind

6 kaffir lime leaves, finely shredded

300 g/10½ oz freshly cooked crabmeat

200 g/7 oz freshly cooked crab claws

150 g/5½ oz canned sweetcorn, drained

1 tbsp of chopped coriander, plus a few sprigs to garnish

salt and pepper

Heat the oil in a large saucepan over a medium heat. Add the garlic and spring onions and cook, stirring, for about 3 minutes, until slightly softened. Add the red peppers and ginger and cook for a further 4 minutes, stirring. Pour in the stock and season with salt and pepper. Bring to the boil, then lower the heat. Pour in the coconut milk, rice wine and lime juice, and stir in the grated lime rind and kaffir lime leaves. Simmer for 15 minutes.

Add the crabmeat and crab claws to the soup with the sweetcorn and coriander. Cook the soup for 15 minutes, until the fish is tender and cooked right through.

Remove from the heat and ladle into serving bowls. Garnish with fresh coriander and serve.

Prawn & Vegetable Bisque

serves 4

3 tbsp butter

1 garlic clove, chopped

1 onion, sliced

1 carrot, peeled and chopped

1 celery stick, trimmed and sliced

1.2 litres/2 pints fish stock

4 tbsp red wine

1 tbsp tomato purée

1 bay leaf

600 g/1 lb 5 oz prawns, peeled and deveined

100 ml/3½ fl oz double cream

salt and pepper

swirls of single cream and whole cooked prawns, to garnish

Melt the butter in a large saucepan over a medium heat. Add the garlic and onion and cook, stirring, for 3 minutes, until slightly softened. Add the carrot and celery and cook for a further 3 minutes, stirring. Pour in the stock and red wine, then add the tomato purée and bay leaf. Season with salt and pepper. Bring to the boil, then lower the heat and simmer for 20 minutes. Remove from the heat and leave to cool for 10 minutes, then remove and discard the bay leaf.

Transfer half of the soup into a food processor and blend until smooth (you may need to do this in batches). Return to the pan with the rest of the soup. Add the prawns and cook over a low heat for 5–6 minutes.

Stir in the cream and cook for a further 2 minutes, then remove from the heat and ladle into serving bowls. Garnish with swirls of single cream and whole cooked prawns and serve at once.

Haddock & Prawn Chowder

serves 4

1 tbsp butter

1 onion, chopped

3 tbsp plain flour

500 ml/18 fl oz fish stock

1 bay leaf

salt and pepper

500 ml/18 fl oz milk

2 tbsp dry white wine

juice and grated rind of 1 lemon

450 g/1 lb haddock fillets, skinned

125 g/4½ oz frozen sweetcorn, defrosted

250 g/9 oz prawns, cooked and peeled

200 ml/7 fl oz double cream

whole cooked prawns, to garnish

fresh green salad, to serve

Melt the butter in a large saucepan over a medium heat. Add the onion and cook, stirring, for about 3 minutes, until slightly softened. In a bowl, mix the flour with enough stock to make a smooth paste and stir it into the pan. Cook, stirring, for 2 minutes, then gradually stir in the remaining stock. Add the bay leaf and season with salt and pepper. Bring to the boil, then lower the heat. Pour in the milk and wine, and stir in the lemon juice and grated rind. Simmer for 15 minutes.

Rinse the haddock under cold running water, then drain and cut into bite-sized chunks. Add them to the soup with the sweetcorn. Cook for 15 minutes, until the fish is tender and cooked through. Stir in the prawns and the cream. Cook for a further 2–3 minutes, then remove from the heat and discard the bay leaf.

Ladle into serving bowls, garnish with whole cooked prawns and serve with a fresh green salad.

Meat

Beef & Vegetable Soup

serves 4

55 g/2 oz pearl barley, rinsed and drained

1.2 litres/2 pints beef stock

1 tsp dried mixed herbs

225 g/8 oz lean rump or sirloin beef

1 large carrot, diced

1 leek, shredded

1 medium onion, chopped

2 celery sticks, sliced

salt and pepper

2 tbsp chopped fresh flat-leaf parsley, to garnish

Place the pearl barley in a large saucepan. Pour over the stock and add the mixed herbs. Bring to the boil, cover and simmer gently over a low heat for 10 minutes.

Meanwhile, trim any fat from the beef and cut the meat into thin strips.

Skim away any scum that has risen to the top of the stock with a flat ladle.

Add the beef, carrot, leek, onion and celery to the pan. Bring back to the boil, cover and simmer for about 1 hour or until the pearl barley, beef and vegetables are just tender.

Skim away any remaining scum that has risen to the top of the soup with a flat ladle. Blot the surface with absorbent kitchen paper to remove any fat. Adjust the seasoning according to taste.

Ladle the soup into warmed bowls, garnish with chopped parsley and serve hot.

Spicy Beef & Noodle Soup

serves 4

1 litre/1¾ pints beef stock

150 ml/5 fl oz vegetable or groundnut oil

85 g/3 oz rice vermicelli noodles

2 shallots, thinly sliced

2 garlic cloves, crushed

2.5-cm/1-inch piece fresh root ginger, thinly sliced

225 g/8 oz piece fillet steak, cut into thin strips

2 tbsp green curry paste

2 tbsp Thai soy sauce

1 tbsp fish sauce

chopped fresh coriander, to garnish

Pour the stock into a large saucepan and bring to the boil. Meanwhile, heat the oil in a wok or large frying pan. Add a third of the noodles and fry for 10–20 seconds, until they have puffed up. Lift out with tongs, drain on kitchen paper and set aside. Discard all but 2 tablespoons of the oil.

Add the shallots, garlic and ginger to the wok or frying pan and stir-fry for 1 minute. Add the beef and curry paste and stir-fry for a further 3–4 minutes, until tender.

Add the beef mixture, the uncooked noodles, soy sauce and fish sauce to the saucepan of stock and simmer for 2–3 minutes, until the noodles have swelled. Serve hot, garnished with the chopped coriander and the reserved crispy noodles.

Beef & Bean Soup

serves 4

2 tbsp vegetable oil

1 large onion, finely chopped

2 garlic cloves, finely chopped

1 green pepper, deseeded and sliced

2 carrots, sliced

400 g/14 oz canned black-eye beans

225 g/8 oz fresh beef mince

1 tsp each ground cumin, chilli powder and paprika

¼ cabbage, sliced

225 g/8 oz tomatoes, peeled and chopped

600 ml/1 pint beef stock

salt and pepper

Heat the oil in a large saucepan over a medium heat. Add the onion and garlic and cook, stirring frequently, for 5 minutes, or until softened. Add the pepper and carrots and cook for a further 5 minutes.

Meanwhile, drain the beans, reserving the liquid from the can. Place two thirds of the beans, reserving the remainder, in a food processor or blender with the bean liquid and process until smooth.

Add the beef to the saucepan and cook, stirring constantly, to break up any lumps, until well browned. Add the spices and cook, stirring, for 2 minutes. Add the cabbage, tomatoes, stock and puréed beans and season to taste with salt and pepper. Bring to the boil, then reduce the heat, cover and simmer for 15 minutes, or until the vegetables are tender.

Stir in the reserved beans, cover and simmer for a further 5 minutes. Ladle the soup into warmed soup bowls and serve.

Beef Consommé with Eggs & Parmesan

serves 4

1.5 litres/2¾ pints beef consommé or beef stock

3 eggs

25 g/1 oz fresh white breadcrumbs

55 g/2 oz Parmesan cheese, freshly grated

salt

Pour the consommé or stock into a saucepan and heat gently, stirring occasionally.

Meanwhile, beat the eggs in a bowl until combined, then stir in the breadcrumbs and Parmesan. Season with salt.

As soon as the consommé or stock comes to the boil, add the egg mixture. When it floats to the surface, stir with a fork to break it up. Ladle into warmed soup bowls and then serve immediately.

Mexican-Style Beef & Rice Soup

serves 4

3 tbsp olive oil

500 g/1 lb 2 oz boneless stewing beef, cut into 2.5-cm/1-inch pieces

150 ml/5 fl oz red wine

1 onion, finely chopped

1 green pepper, deseeded and finely chopped

1 small fresh red chilli, deseeded and finely chopped

2 garlic cloves, finely chopped

1 carrot, finely chopped

¼ tsp ground coriander

¼ tsp ground cumin

⅛ tsp ground cinnamon

¼ tsp dried oregano

1 bay leaf

grated rind of ½ orange

400 g/14 oz canned chopped tomatoes

1.2 litres/2 pints beef stock

50 g/1¾ oz long-grain white rice

25 g/1 oz raisins

15 g/½ oz plain chocolate, melted

Heat half the oil in a large frying pan over a medium-high heat. Add the meat in one layer and cook until well browned, turning to colour all sides. Remove the pan from the heat and pour in the wine.

Heat the remaining oil in a large saucepan over a medium heat. Add the onion, cover and cook for about 3 minutes, stirring occasionally, until just softened. Add the green pepper, chilli, garlic and carrot, and continue cooking, covered, for 3 minutes.

Add the coriander, cumin, cinnamon, oregano, bay leaf and orange rind. Stir in the tomatoes and stock, along with the beef and wine. Bring almost to the boil and when the mixture begins to bubble, reduce the heat to low. Cover and simmer gently, stirring occasionally, for about 1 hour until the meat is tender.

Stir in the rice, raisins and chocolate, and continue cooking, stirring occasionally, for about 30 minutes until the rice is tender.

Ladle into warmed bowls and serve.

Beef Broth with Herbs & Vegetables

serves 4–6

200 g/7 oz celeriac, peeled and finely diced

2 large carrots, finely diced

2 tsp chopped fresh marjoram leaves

2 tsp chopped fresh parsley

2 plum tomatoes, skinned, deseeded and diced

salt and pepper

for the beef stock

550 g/1 lb 4 oz boneless beef shin or stewing steak, cut into large cubes

750 g/1 lb 10 oz veal, beef or pork bones

2 onions, quartered

2.5 litres/4⅓ pints water

4 garlic cloves, sliced

2 carrots, sliced

1 large leek, sliced

1 celery stick, cut into 5-cm/2.5-inch pieces

1 bay leaf

4–5 sprigs of fresh thyme, or ¼ tsp dried thyme

salt

Preheat the oven to 190°C/375°F/Gas Mark 5. To make the stock, trim any fat from the beef and put in a roasting tin with the bones and onions. Roast in the oven for 30–40 minutes, turning once or twice. Transfer to a flameproof casserole and discard the fat.

Add the water and bring to the boil. Skim off any scrum that rises to the surface. Reduce the heat and add the garlic, carrots, leek, celery, bay leaf, thyme and salt. Simmer, uncovered for 4 hours. Do not stir. If the ingredients emerge from the liquid, top up with water.

Gently ladle the stock through a muslin-lined sieve into a large container and remove as much fat as possible. Save the meat for another purpose, if wished, and discard the bones and vegetables. (There should be about 2 litres/3½ pints of stock.)

Boil the stock very gently until it is reduced to 1.5 litres/ 2¾ pints, or if the stock already has concentrated flavour, measure out that amount and reserve the remainder. Taste and adjust the seasoning if necessary.

Bring a saucepan of salted water to the boil and add the celeriac and carrots. Reduce the heat, cover and simmer for 15 minutes. Drain.

Add the marjoram and parsley to the boiling beef stock. Divide the cooked vegetables and diced tomatoes among warmed bowls, ladle over the boiling stock and serve.

Chunky Potato & Beef Soup

serves 4

2 tbsp vegetable oil

225 g/8 oz lean braising or frying steak, cut into strips

225 g/8 oz new potatoes, halved

1 carrot, diced

2 celery sticks, sliced

2 leeks, sliced

850 ml/1½ pints beef stock

8 baby sweetcorn cobs, sliced

1 bouquet garni

2 tbsp dry sherry

salt and pepper

chopped fresh flat-leaf parsley, to garnish

Heat the vegetable oil in a large saucepan. Add the strips of meat to the saucepan and cook for 3 minutes, turning constantly. Add the potatoes, carrot, celery and leeks to the saucepan. Cook for a further 5 minutes, stirring.

Pour the beef stock into the saucepan and bring to the boil. Reduce the heat until the liquid is simmering, then add the baby sweetcorn cobs and the bouquet garni. Cook for a further 20 minutes, or until cooked through.

Remove and discard the bouquet garni. Stir the dry sherry into the soup, then season to taste.

Ladle the soup into warmed bowls, garnish with chopped parsley and serve.

Asian Lamb Soup

serves 4

150 g/5½ oz lean tender lamb, such as neck fillet or leg steak

2 garlic cloves, very finely chopped

2 tbsp soy sauce

1.2 litres/2 pints chicken stock

1 tbsp grated fresh root ginger

5-cm/2-inch piece lemon grass, sliced into very thin rounds

¼ tsp chilli purée, or to taste

6–8 cherry tomatoes, quartered

4 spring onions, sliced finely

50 g/1¾ oz beansprouts, snapped in half

2 tbsp fresh coriander leaves

1 tsp olive oil

Trim all visible fat from the lamb and slice the meat thinly. Cut the slices into bite-sized pieces. Spread the meat in one layer on a plate and sprinkle over the garlic and 1 tablespoon of the soy sauce. Leave to marinate, covered, for at least 10 minutes or up to 1 hour.

Put the stock in a saucepan with the ginger, lemon grass, remaining soy sauce and the chilli purée. Bring just to the boil, reduce the heat, cover and simmer for 10–15 minutes.

When ready to serve the soup, drop the tomatoes, spring onions, beansprouts and fresh coriander leaves into the simmering stock.

Heat the oil in a frying pan and add the lamb with its marinade. Stir-fry the lamb just until it is no longer red and divide among warmed bowls.

Ladle over the hot stock and serve immediately.

Scotch Broth

serves 4

1 tbsp vegetable oil

500 g/1 lb 2 oz lean neck of lamb

1 large onion, sliced

2 carrots, sliced

2 leeks, sliced

1 litre/1¾ pints vegetable stock

1 bay leaf

sprigs of fresh parsley

55 g/2 oz pearl barley, rinsed and drained

salt and pepper

Heat the vegetable oil in a large, heavy-based saucepan and add the pieces of lamb, turning them to seal and brown on both sides. Lift the lamb out of the pan and set aside until required.

Add the onion, carrots and leeks to the saucepan and cook gently for about 3 minutes.

Return the lamb to the saucepan and add the vegetable stock, bay leaf, parsley and pearl barley to the saucepan. Bring the mixture in the pan to the boil, then reduce the heat. Cover and simmer for 1½–2 hours.

Discard the parsley sprigs. Lift the pieces of lamb from the broth and allow them to cool slightly. Remove the bones and any fat and chop the meat. Return the lamb to the broth and reheat gently. Season to taste with salt and pepper.

It is advisable to prepare this soup a day ahead, then leave it to cool, cover and refrigerate overnight. When ready to serve, remove and discard the layer of fat from the surface and reheat the soup gently. Ladle into warmed bowls and serve immediately.

Spicy Lamb Soup with Chickpeas & Courgettes

serves 4–6

1–2 tbsp olive oil

450 g/1 lb lean boneless lamb, trimmed of fat and cut into 1-cm/½-inch cubes

1 onion, finely chopped

2–3 garlic cloves, crushed

1.2 litres/2 pints water

400 g/14 oz canned chopped tomatoes

1 bay leaf

½ tsp each of dried thyme and oregano

⅛ tsp ground cinnamon

¼ tsp each of ground cumin and turmeric

1 tsp harissa

400 g/14 oz canned chickpeas, rinsed and drained

1 each of carrot, potato and courgette, diced

100 g/3½ oz fresh peas

fresh mint sprigs, to garnish

Heat 1 tablespoon of the oil in a large saucepan or cast-iron casserole over a medium-high heat. Add the lamb, in batches if necessary to avoid crowding the pan, and cook until evenly browned on all sides, adding a little more oil if needed. Remove the meat with a slotted spoon when browned.

Reduce the heat and add the onion and garlic to the pan. Cook, stirring frequently, for 1–2 minutes.

Add the water and return all the meat to the pan. Bring just to the boil and skim off any scum that rises to the surface. Reduce the heat and stir in the tomatoes, bay leaf, thyme, oregano, cinnamon, cumin, turmeric and harissa. Simmer for about 1 hour, or until the meat is very tender. Discard the bay leaf.

Stir in the chickpeas, carrot and potato and simmer for 15 minutes. Add the courgette and peas and continue simmering for 15–20 minutes, or until all the vegetables are tender.

Ladle the soup into warmed bowls and garnish with mint.

Lamb & Rice Soup

serves 4

150 g/5½ oz lean lamb

50 g/1¾ oz rice

850 ml/1½ pints lamb stock

1 leek, sliced

1 garlic clove, thinly sliced

2 tsp light soy sauce

1 tsp rice wine vinegar

1 medium open-cap mushroom, thinly sliced

salt

Using a sharp knife, trim any fat from the lamb and cut the meat into thin strips. Set aside until required.

Bring a large pan of lightly salted water to the boil and add the rice. Bring back to the boil, stir once, reduce the heat and cook for 10–15 minutes, until tender. Drain the cooked rice, rinse under cold running water, drain again and set aside.

Put the lamb stock in a large saucepan and bring to the boil. Add the lamb strips, leek, garlic, soy sauce and rice wine vinegar, reduce the heat, cover and simmer for 10 minutes, or until the lamb is tender and cooked through.

Add the mushroom slices and cooked rice to the saucepan and cook for a further 2–3 minutes, or until the mushroom is completely cooked through.

Ladle the soup into warmed bowls and serve immediately.

Split Pea & Ham Soup

serves 6–8

500 g/1 lb 2 oz split green peas

1 tbsp olive oil

1 large onion, finely chopped

1 large carrot, finely chopped

1 celery stick, finely chopped

1 litre/1¾ pints chicken or vegetable stock

1 litre/1¾ pints water

225 g/8 oz lean smoked ham, finely diced

¼ tsp dried thyme

¼ tsp dried marjoram

1 bay leaf

salt and pepper

Rinse the peas under cold running water. Put in a saucepan and cover generously with water. Bring to the boil and boil for 3 minutes, skimming off the scum from the surface. Drain the peas.

Heat the oil in a large saucepan over a medium heat. Add the onion and cook for 3–4 minutes, stirring occasionally, until just softened.

Add the carrot and celery and continue cooking for 2 minutes. Add the peas, pour over the stock and water and stir to combine.

Bring just to the boil and stir the ham into the soup. Add the thyme, marjoram and bay leaf. Reduce the heat, cover and cook gently for 1–1½ hours, until the ingredients are very soft. Remove the bay leaf.

Taste and adjust the seasoning. Ladle into warmed soup bowls and serve.

Cheese & Bacon Soup

serves 4

2 tbsp butter

2 garlic cloves, chopped

1 large onion, sliced

250 g/9 oz smoked lean back bacon, chopped

2 large leeks, trimmed and sliced

2 tbsp plain flour

1 litre/1¾ pints vegetable stock

450 g/1 lb potatoes, chopped

100 ml/3½ fl oz double cream

300 g/10½ oz grated Cheddar cheese, plus extra to garnish

salt and pepper

Melt the butter in a large saucepan over a medium heat. Add the garlic and onion and cook, stirring, for 3 minutes, until slightly softened. Add the chopped bacon and leeks and cook for a further 3 minutes, stirring.

In a bowl, mix the flour with enough stock to make a smooth paste, then stir it into the pan. Cook, stirring, for 2 minutes. Pour in the remaining stock, then add the potatoes. Season with salt and pepper. Bring the soup to the boil, then lower the heat and simmer gently for 25 minutes, until the potatoes are tender and cooked through.

Stir in the cream and cook for 5 minutes, then gradually stir in the cheese until melted. Remove from the heat and ladle into serving bowls. Garnish with grated Cheddar cheese and serve immediately.

Sausage & Red Cabbage Soup

serves 4

2 tbsp olive oil

1 garlic clove, chopped

1 large onion, chopped

1 large leek, sliced

2 tbsp cornflour

1 litre/1¾ pints vegetable stock

450 g/1 lb potatoes, sliced

200 g/7 oz skinless sausages, sliced

150 g/5½ oz red cabbage, chopped

200 g/7 oz canned black-eye beans, drained

125 ml/4 fl oz double cream

salt and pepper

ground paprika, to garnish

Heat the oil in a large saucepan. Add the garlic and onion and cook over a medium heat, stirring, for 3 minutes, until slightly softened. Add the leek and cook for a further 3 minutes, stirring.

In a bowl, mix the cornflour with enough stock to make a smooth paste, then stir it into the pan. Cook, stirring, for 2 minutes. Stir in the remaining stock, then add the potatoes and sausages. Season with salt and pepper. Bring to the boil, then lower the heat and simmer for 25 minutes.

Add the red cabbage and beans and cook for 10 minutes, then stir in the cream and cook for a further 5 minutes. Remove from the heat and ladle into serving bowls. Garnish with ground paprika and serve immediately.

Pork & Vegetable Broth

serves 4

1 tbsp chilli oil

1 garlic clove, chopped

3 spring onions, sliced

1 red pepper, deseeded and finely sliced

2 tbsp cornflour

1 litre/1¾ pints vegetable stock

1 tbsp soy sauce

2 tbsp rice wine or dry sherry

150 g/5½ oz pork fillet, sliced

1 tbsp finely chopped lemon grass

1 small red chilli, deseeded and finely chopped

1 tbsp grated fresh root ginger

115 g/4 oz fine egg noodles

200 g/7 oz canned water chestnuts, drained and sliced

salt and pepper

Heat the oil in a large saucepan. Add the garlic and spring onions and cook over a medium heat, stirring, for 3 minutes, until slightly softened. Add the red pepper and cook for a further 5 minutes, stirring.

In a bowl, mix the cornflour with enough of the stock to make a smooth paste, then stir it into the pan. Cook, stirring, for 2 minutes. Stir in the remaining stock and the soy sauce and rice wine, then add the pork, lemon grass, chilli and ginger. Season with salt and pepper. Bring to the boil, then lower the heat and simmer for 25 minutes.

Bring a separate saucepan of water to the boil, add the noodles and cook for 3 minutes. Remove from the heat, drain, then add the noodles to the soup along with the water chestnuts. Cook for a further 2 minutes, then remove from the heat and ladle into warmed bowls.

Pork Chilli Soup

serves 4

2 tsp olive oil

500 g/1 lb 2 oz fresh lean pork mince

1 onion, finely chopped

1 celery stick, finely chopped

1 red pepper, cored, deseeded and finely chopped

2–3 garlic cloves, finely chopped

3 tbsp tomato purée

400 g/14 oz canned chopped tomatoes

450 ml/16 fl oz chicken or meat stock

1/8 tsp ground coriander

1/8 tsp ground cumin

1/4 tsp dried oregano

1 tsp mild chilli powder, to taste

salt and pepper

soured cream, to serve

Heat the oil in a large saucepan over a medium-high heat. Add the pork, season with salt and pepper, and cook until no longer pink, stirring frequently. Reduce the heat to medium and add the onion, celery, red pepper and garlic. Cover and continue cooking for 5 minutes, stirring occasionally, until the onion is softened.

Add the tomato purée, tomatoes and the stock. Add the coriander, cumin, oregano and chilli powder. Stir the ingredients in to combine well.

Bring just to the boil, reduce the heat to low, cover and simmer for 30–40 minutes until all the vegetables are very tender. Taste and adjust the seasoning, adding more chilli powder if you like it hotter.

Ladle the soup into warmed bowls and serve with a spoonful of soured cream.

Chorizo & Red Kidney Bean Soup

serves 4

2 tbsp olive oil

2 garlic cloves, chopped

2 red onions, chopped

1 red pepper, deseeded and chopped

2 tbsp cornflour

1 litre/1¾ pints vegetable stock

450 g/1 lb potatoes, peeled, halved and sliced

150 g/5½ oz chorizo, sliced

2 courgettes, trimmed and sliced

200 g/7 oz canned red kidney beans, drained

125 ml/4 fl oz double cream

salt and pepper

Heat the oil in a large saucepan. Add the garlic and onions and cook over a medium heat, stirring, for 3 minutes, until slightly softened. Add the red pepper and cook for a further 3 minutes, stirring. In a bowl, mix the cornflour with enough stock to make a smooth paste and stir it into the pan. Cook, stirring, for 2 minutes. Stir in the remaining stock, then add the potatoes and season with salt and pepper. Bring to the boil, then lower the heat and simmer for 25 minutes, until the vegetables are tender.

Add the chorizo, courgettes and kidney beans to the pan. Cook for 10 minutes, then stir in the cream and cook for a further 5 minutes. Remove from the heat and ladle into serving bowls.

Bacon & Lentil Soup

serves 4

450 g/1 lb thick, rindless smoked bacon rashers, diced

1 onion, chopped

2 carrots, sliced

2 celery sticks, chopped

1 turnip, chopped

1 large potato, chopped

85 g/3 oz Puy lentils

1 bouquet garni

1 litre/1¾ pints water or chicken stock

salt and pepper

Heat a large, heavy-based saucepan or flameproof casserole. Add the bacon and cook over a medium heat, stirring, for 4–5 minutes, or until the fat runs. Add the chopped onion, carrots, celery, turnip and potato and cook, stirring frequently, for 5 minutes.

Add the lentils and bouquet garni and pour in the water. Bring to the boil, reduce the heat and simmer for 1 hour, or until the lentils are tender.

Remove and discard the bouquet garni and season the soup to taste with pepper, and with salt, if necessary. Remove from the heat, ladle into warmed bowls and serve.

Chicken &
Poultry

Cream of Chicken Soup

serves 4

3 tbsp butter

4 shallots, chopped

1 leek, sliced

450 g/1 lb skinless chicken breasts, chopped

600 ml/1 pint chicken stock

1 tbsp chopped fresh parsley

1 tbsp chopped fresh thyme, plus extra sprigs to garnish

175 ml/6 fl oz double cream

salt and pepper

Melt the butter in a large saucepan over a medium heat. Add the shallots and cook, stirring, for 3 minutes, until slightly softened. Add the leek and cook for a further 5 minutes, stirring. Add the chicken, stock and herbs, and season with salt and pepper. Bring to the boil, then lower the heat and simmer for 25 minutes, until the chicken is tender and cooked through. Remove from the heat and leave to cool for 10 minutes.

Transfer the soup to a food processor or blender and process until smooth (you may need to do this in batches). Return the soup to the rinsed-out pan and warm over a low heat for 5 minutes.

Stir in the cream and cook for a further 2 minutes, then remove from the heat and ladle into serving bowls. Garnish with sprigs of thyme and serve immediately.

Chicken, Rice & Vegetable Soup

serves 4

1.5 litres/2¾ pints chicken stock

2 small carrots, very thinly sliced

1 celery stick, finely diced

1 baby leek, halved lengthways and thinly sliced

115 g/4 oz petit pois, defrosted if frozen

175 g/6 oz cooked rice

150 g/5½ oz cooked chicken, sliced

2 tsp chopped fresh tarragon

1 tbsp chopped fresh flat-leaf parsley, plus extra sprigs to garnish

Put the stock in a large saucepan and add the carrots, celery and leek. Bring to the boil, reduce the heat to low and simmer gently, partially covered, for 10 minutes.

Stir in the petit pois, rice and chicken and continue cooking for a further 10–15 minutes, or until the vegetables are tender.

Add the chopped tarragon and parsley, then taste and adjust the seasoning, adding salt and pepper as needed.

Ladle the soup into warmed bowls, garnish with parsley and serve.

Chicken Noodle Soup

serves 4–6

2 skinless chicken breasts

1.2 litres/2 pints water or chicken stock

3 carrots, peeled and sliced into 5-mm/¼-inch slices

85 g/3 oz vermicelli (or other small noodles)

salt and pepper

fresh tarragon leaves, to garnish

Place the chicken breasts in a large saucepan, add the water and bring to a simmer. Cook for 25–30 minutes. Skim any foam from the surface if necessary. Remove the chicken from the stock and keep warm.

Continue to simmer the stock, add the carrots and vermicelli and cook for 4–5 minutes.

Thinly slice or shred the chicken breasts and place in warmed serving dishes.

Season the soup to taste with salt and pepper and pour over the chicken. Serve at once garnished with the tarragon.

Chicken & Potato Soup with Bacon

serves 4

1 tbsp butter

2 garlic cloves, chopped

1 onion, sliced

250 g/9 oz smoked lean back bacon, chopped

2 large leeks, sliced

2 tbsp plain flour

1 litre/1¾ pints chicken stock

800 g/1 lb 12 oz potatoes, chopped

200 g/7 oz skinless chicken breast, chopped

4 tbsp double cream

salt and pepper

grilled bacon and sprigs of flat-leaf parsley, to garnish

Melt the butter in a large saucepan over a medium heat. Add the garlic and onion and cook, stirring, for 3 minutes, until slightly softened. Add the chopped bacon and leeks and cook for a further 3 minutes, stirring.

In a bowl, mix the flour with enough stock to make a smooth paste, then stir it into the pan. Cook, stirring, for 2 minutes. Pour in the remaining stock, then add the potatoes and chicken. Season with salt and pepper. Bring to the boil, then lower the heat and simmer for 25 minutes, until the chicken and potatoes are tender and cooked through.

Stir in the cream and cook for a further 2 minutes, then remove from the heat and ladle into serving bowls. Garnish with the grilled bacon and flat-leaf parsley, and serve immediately.

Chicken Gumbo Soup

serves 6

2 tbsp olive oil

4 tbsp plain flour

1 onion, finely chopped

1 small green pepper, deseeded and finely chopped

1 celery stick, finely chopped

1.2 litres/2 pints chicken stock

400 g/14 oz canned chopped tomatoes

3 garlic cloves, finely chopped or crushed

125 g/4½ oz okra, stems removed, cut into 5-mm/ ¼-inch thick slices

50 g/1¾ oz white rice

200 g/7 oz cooked chicken, cubed

115 g/4 oz cooked garlic sausage, sliced or cubed

salt and pepper

Heat the oil in a large heavy-based saucepan over a medium-low heat and stir in the flour. Cook for about 15 minutes, stirring occasionally, until the mixture is a rich golden brown.

Add the onion, green pepper and celery and continue cooking for about 10 minutes until the onion softens.

Slowly pour in the stock and bring to the boil, stirring well and scraping the bottom of the pan to mix in the flour. Remove the pan from the heat.

Add the tomatoes and garlic. Stir in the okra and rice and season to taste with salt and pepper. Reduce the heat, cover and simmer for 20 minutes, or until the okra is tender.

Add the chicken and sausage and continue simmering for about 10 minutes. Taste and adjust the seasoning, if necessary, and ladle into warmed bowls to serve.

Mulligatawny Soup

serves 4–6

55 g/2 oz butter

2 onions, chopped

1 small turnip, cut into small dice

2 carrots, finely sliced

1 Cox's apple, cored, peeled and chopped

2 tbsp mild curry powder

1.2 litres/2 pints chicken stock

juice of ½ lemon

175 g/6 oz cold cooked chicken, cut into small pieces

2 tbsp chopped fresh coriander, plus extra to garnish

salt and pepper

55 g/2 oz cooked rice, to serve

Melt the butter in a large saucepan over a medium heat, add the onions and sauté gently until soft but not brown.

Add the turnip, carrots and apple and continue to cook for a further 3–4 minutes.

Stir in the curry powder until the vegetables are well coated, then pour in the stock. Bring to the boil, cover and simmer for about 45 minutes. Season well with salt and pepper to taste and add the lemon juice.

Transfer the soup to a food processor or blender. Process until smooth and return to the rinsed-out saucepan. Add the chicken and coriander to the saucepan and heat through.

Place a spoonful of rice in each serving bowl and pour the soup over the top. Garnish with coriander and serve.

Thai Chicken-Coconut Soup

serves 4

115 g/4 oz dried cellophane noodles

1.2 litres/2 pints chicken or vegetable stock

1 lemon grass stalk, crushed

1-cm/½-inch piece fresh root ginger, peeled and very finely chopped

2 fresh kaffir lime leaves, thinly sliced

1 fresh red chilli, or to taste, deseeded and thinly sliced

2 skinless, boneless chicken breasts, thinly sliced

200 ml/7 fl oz coconut cream

2 tbsp nam pla (Thai fish sauce)

1 tbsp fresh lime juice

55 g/2 oz beansprouts

4 spring onions, green part only, finely sliced

fresh coriander leaves, to garnish

Soak the dried noodles in a large bowl with enough lukewarm water to cover for 20 minutes, until soft. Alternatively, cook according to the packet instructions. Drain well and set aside.

Meanwhile, bring the stock to the boil in a large saucepan over a high heat. Lower the heat, add the lemon grass, ginger, lime leaves and chilli and simmer for 5 minutes. Add the chicken and continue simmering for a further 3 minutes, or until cooked. Stir in the coconut cream, nam pla and lime juice and continue simmering for 3 minutes. Add the beansprouts and spring onions and simmer for a further 1 minute. Taste and gradually add extra nam pla or lime juice at this point, if needed. Remove and discard the lemon grass stalk.

Divide the vermicelli noodles between warmed bowls. Bring the soup back to the boil, then ladle into each bowl. The heat of the soup will warm the noodles. Garnish with coriander leaves and serve.

Chicken Ravioli in Tarragon Broth

serves 6

2 litres/3½ pints chicken
stock

2 tbsp finely chopped fresh
tarragon leaves

freshly grated Parmesan
cheese, to serve

for the pasta dough

125 g/4½ oz flour, plus
extra if needed

2 tbsp fresh tarragon
leaves, stems removed

1 egg

1 egg, separated

1 tsp extra virgin olive oil

2–3 tbsp water

pinch of salt

for the filling

200 g/7 oz cooked chicken,
coarsely chopped

½ tsp grated lemon rind

2 tbsp chopped mixed fresh
tarragon, chives and
parsley

4 tbsp whipping cream

salt and pepper

To make the pasta, combine the flour, tarragon and salt in a food processor. Beat together the egg, egg yolk, oil and 2 tablespoons of water. With the machine running, pour in the egg mixture and process until it forms a ball. Wrap and chill for at least 30 minutes. Reserve the egg white.

To make the filling, put the chicken, lemon rind and mixed herbs in a food processor and season with salt and pepper. Chop finely, by pulsing; do not overprocess. Scrape into a bowl and stir in the cream. Taste and adjust the seasoning.

Divide the pasta dough in half. Cover one half and roll out the other half on a floured surface as thinly as possible, less than 1.5 mm/¹⁄₁₆ inch. Cut out rectangles measuring about 10 x 5 cm/4 x 2 inches.

Place a teaspoon of filling on one half of each rectangle. Brush the edges with egg white and fold in half. Press the edge to seal. Arrange the ravioli on a baking sheet dusted with flour. Repeat with the remaining dough. Allow the ravioli to dry for about 15 minutes or chill for 1–2 hours.

Bring a large quantity of water to the boil. Drop in half of the ravioli and cook for 12–15 minutes, until just tender. Drain on a clean tea towel while cooking the remainder.

Meanwhile, put the stock and tarragon in a large saucepan. Bring to the boil, then cover and simmer for 15 minutes. Add the ravioli and simmer for a further 5 minutes. Ladle into warmed bowls and serve with Parmesan cheese.

Chicken, Mushroom & Barley Soup

serves 4

75 g/2¾ oz pearl barley, rinsed and drained

2 tbsp butter

1 large onion, sliced

1 large leek, trimmed and sliced

1 litre/1¾ pints chicken stock

450 g/1 lb skinless chicken breasts, chopped

250 g/9 oz chestnut mushrooms, sliced

1 large carrot, peeled and chopped

1 tbsp chopped fresh oregano

1 bay leaf

salt and pepper

sprigs of fresh flat-leaf parsley, to garnish

fresh crusty bread, to serve

Bring a saucepan of water to the boil. Add the barley and boil over a high heat for 5 minutes, skimming the surface when necessary. Remove from the heat and reserve.

Melt the butter in a large saucepan. Add the onion and cook over a medium heat, stirring, for 3 minutes, until slightly softened. Add the leek and cook for a further 4 minutes, stirring. Stir in the stock, then drain the barley and add to the pan. Season with salt and pepper. Bring to the boil, then lower the heat and simmer for 45 minutes. Add the chicken, mushrooms, carrot, oregano and bay leaf. Cook for a further 30 minutes.

Remove from the heat and discard the bay leaf. Ladle into serving bowls, garnish with sprigs of fresh flat-leaf parsley and serve with fresh crusty bread.

Chicken, Leek & Prune Soup

serves 4–6

25 g/1 oz butter

350 g/12 oz boneless chicken, diced

350 g/12 oz leeks, cut into 2.5-cm/1-inch pieces

1.2 litres/2 pints chicken stock

1 bouquet garni

8 pitted prunes, halved

70 g/2¼ oz cooked rice

1 red pepper, diced (optional)

salt and white pepper

Melt the butter in a large saucepan. Add the chicken and leeks and cook for 8 minutes.

Add the chicken stock and bouquet garni sachet to the saucepan and stir well, then season with salt and pepper to taste. Bring to the boil and simmer for 45 minutes.

Add the prunes to the saucepan with the cooked rice and diced pepper, if using, and simmer for about 20 minutes.

Remove the bouquet garni from the soup and discard. Ladle into warmed soup bowls and serve immediately.

Cock-a-leekie

serves 6

1.3 kg/3 lb chicken

2.25 litres/4 pints beef stock

900 g/2 lb leeks

1 bouquet garni

450 g/1 lb prunes, stoned and soaked overnight in enough cold water to cover

salt and pepper

Put the chicken, breast-side down, in a large, heavy-based saucepan or flameproof casserole. Pour in the stock and bring to the boil, skimming off any froth that rises to the surface.

Tie half the leeks together in a bundle with kitchen string and thinly slice the remainder. Add the bundle of leeks to the saucepan with the bouquet garni and a pinch of salt, reduce the heat, partially cover and simmer for 2 hours, or until the chicken is tender.

Remove and discard the bundle of leeks and bouquet garni. Drain the prunes, add them to the saucepan and simmer for 20 minutes. Season to taste with salt and pepper and add the sliced leeks. Simmer for a further 10 minutes. Slice the chicken, or cut into bite-sized pieces, and serve immediately.

Turkey Soup with Rice, Mushrooms & Sage

serves 4–5

3 tbsp butter

1 onion, finely chopped

1 celery stick, finely chopped

25 large fresh sage leaves, finely chopped

4 tbsp plain flour

1.2 litres/2 pints turkey or chicken stock

100 g/3½ oz brown rice

250 g/9 oz mushrooms, sliced

200 g/7 oz cooked turkey, diced

200 ml/7 fl oz double cream

salt and pepper

sprigs of fresh sage, to garnish

freshly grated Parmesan cheese, to serve

Melt half the butter in a large saucepan over a medium-low heat. Add the onion, celery and sage and cook for 3–4 minutes, until the onion is softened, stirring frequently. Stir in the flour and continue cooking for 2 minutes.

Slowly add about one quarter of the stock and stir well, scraping the bottom of the pan to mix in the flour. Pour in the remaining stock, stirring to combine completely, and bring just to the boil.

Stir in the rice and season with salt and pepper. Reduce the heat and simmer gently, partially covered, for about 30 minutes until the rice is just tender, stirring occasionally.

Meanwhile, melt the remaining butter in a large frying pan over a medium heat. Add the mushrooms and season with salt and pepper. Cook for about 8 minutes, until they are golden brown, stirring occasionally at first, then more often after they start to colour. Add the mushrooms to the soup.

Add the turkey to the soup and stir in the cream. Continue simmering for about 10 minutes, until heated through. Taste and adjust the seasoning, if necessary. Ladle into warmed bowls, garnish with sage and serve with Parmesan cheese.

Turkey & Lentil Soup

serves 4

1 tbsp olive oil

1 garlic clove, chopped

1 large onion, chopped

200 g/7 oz mushrooms, sliced

1 red pepper, deseeded and chopped

6 tomatoes, skinned, deseeded and chopped

1.2 litre/2 pints chicken stock

150 ml/5 fl oz red wine

85 g/3 oz cauliflower florets

1 carrot, peeled and chopped

200 g/7 oz red lentils

350 g/12 oz cooked turkey meat, chopped

1 courgette, trimmed and chopped

1 tbsp shredded fresh basil

basil leaves, to garnish

salt and pepper

thick slices of fresh crusty bread, to serve

Heat the oil in a large saucepan. Add the garlic and onion and cook over a medium heat, stirring, for 3 minutes, until slightly softened. Add the mushrooms, red pepper and tomatoes and cook for a further 5 minutes, stirring. Pour in the stock and red wine, then add the cauliflower, carrot and red lentils. Season with salt and pepper. Bring to the boil, then lower the heat and simmer the soup gently for 25 minutes, until the vegetables are tender and cooked through.

Add the turkey and courgette to the pan and cook for 10 minutes. Stir in the shredded basil and cook for a further 5 minutes, then remove from the heat and ladle into serving bowls. Garnish with basil leaves and serve with fresh crusty bread.

Turkey, Leek & Stilton Soup

serves 4

4 tbsp butter

1 large onion, chopped

1 leek, trimmed and sliced

325 g/11½ oz cooked turkey meat, sliced

600 ml/1 pint chicken stock

150 g/5½ oz Stilton cheese, crumbled

150 ml/5 fl oz double cream

1 tbsp chopped fresh tarragon

pepper

fresh tarragon leaves and croûtons, to garnish

Melt the butter in a saucepan over a medium heat. Add the onion and cook, stirring, for 4 minutes, until slightly softened. Add the leek and cook for another 3 minutes.

Add the turkey to the pan and pour in the stock. Bring to the boil, then reduce the heat and simmer gently, stirring occasionally, for about 15 minutes. Remove from the heat and leave to cool a little.

Transfer half of the soup into a food processor and blend until smooth. Return the mixture to the pan with the rest of the soup, stir in the Stilton, cream and tarragon and season with pepper. Reheat gently, stirring. Remove from the heat, ladle into warmed soup bowls, garnish with tarragon and croûtons and serve.

Lemon Turkey Soup with Mushrooms

serves 4

350 g/12 oz boneless turkey, cut into 1-cm/½-inch pieces

1 litre/1¾ pints chicken stock

l onion, quartered

2 carrots, thinly sliced

2 garlic cloves, halved

1 pared strip lemon rind

1 bay leaf

1 tbsp butter

350 g/12 oz small button mushrooms, quartered

4 tbsp cornflour

125 ml/4 fl oz double cream

freshly grated nutmeg

fresh lemon juice, to taste (optional)

1–2 tbsp chopped fresh flat-leaf parsley

salt and pepper

Put the turkey in a large saucepan and add the stock. Bring just to the boil and skim off any scum that rises to the surface.

Add the onion, carrots, garlic, lemon rind and bay leaf. Season with salt and pepper. Reduce the heat and simmer, partially covered, for about 45 minutes, stirring occasionally, until the turkey is cooked.

Remove the turkey and carrots with a slotted spoon and reserve, covered. Strain the stock into a clean saucepan. Discard the onion and garlic, lemon rind and bay leaf.

Melt the butter in a frying pan over a medium-high heat. Add the mushrooms, season, and fry gently until lightly golden. Reserve with the turkey and carrots.

Mix together the cornflour and cream. Bring the cooking liquid just to the boil and whisk in the cream mixture. Boil very gently for 2–3 minutes until it thickens, whisking almost constantly.

Add the reserved meat and vegetables to the soup and simmer over a low heat for about 5 minutes until heated through. Taste and adjust the seasoning, adding nutmeg and a squeeze of lemon juice, if using. Stir in the parsley, then ladle into warmed bowls and serve.

Oriental Duck Broth

serves 4–6

2 duck leg quarters, skinned

1 litre/1¾ pints water

600 ml/1 pint chicken stock

2.5-cm/1-inch piece fresh root ginger, sliced

1 large carrot, sliced

1 onion, sliced

1 leek, sliced

3 garlic cloves, crushed

l tsp black peppercorns

2 tbsp soy sauce, or to taste

l small carrot, cut into thin strips or slivers

l small leek, cut into thin strips or slivers

100 g/3½ oz shiitake mushrooms, thinly sliced

25 g/1 oz watercress leaves

salt and pepper

Put the duck in a large saucepan with the water. Bring just to the boil and skim off the scum that rises to the surface. Add the stock, ginger, carrot, onion, leek, garlic, peppercorns and soy sauce. Reduce the heat and simmer, partially covered, for 1½ hours.

Remove the duck from the stock and set aside. When the duck is cool enough to handle, remove the meat from the bones and slice thinly or shred into bite-sized pieces, discarding any fat.

Strain the stock and press the vegetables with the back of a spoon to extract all the liquid. Remove as much fat as possible. Discard the vegetables and herbs.

Bring the stock just to the boil in a clean saucepan and add the strips of carrot and leek, the mushrooms and duck meat. Reduce the heat and cook gently for 5 minutes, or until the carrot is just tender.

Stir in the watercress and continue simmering for 1–2 minutes until it is wilted. Taste the soup and adjust the seasoning if needed, adding a little more soy sauce if wished. Ladle the soup into warmed bowls and serve immediately.

Duck with Spring Onion Soup

serves 4

2 duck breasts, skin on

2 tbsp red curry paste

2 tbsp vegetable or groundnut oil

bunch of spring onions, chopped

2 garlic cloves, crushed

5-cm/2-inch piece fresh root ginger, grated

2 carrots, thinly sliced

1 red pepper, deseeded and cut into strips

1 litre/1¼ pints chicken stock

2 tbsp sweet chilli sauce

3–4 tbsp Thai soy sauce

400 g/14 oz canned straw mushrooms, drained

Slash the skin of the duck 3 or 4 times with a sharp knife and rub in the curry paste. Cook the duck breasts, skin-side down, in a wok or frying pan over a high heat for 2–3 minutes. Turn over, reduce the heat and cook for a further 3–4 minutes, until cooked through. Lift out and slice thickly. Set aside and keep warm.

Meanwhile, heat the oil in a wok or large frying pan and stir-fry half the spring onions, the garlic, ginger, carrots and red pepper for 2–3 minutes. Pour in the stock and add the chilli sauce, soy sauce and mushrooms. Bring to the boil, lower the heat and simmer for 4–5 minutes.

Ladle the soup into warmed bowls, top with the duck slices and garnish with the remaining spring onions. Serve immediately.

Oriental Chicken Balls & Greens in Broth

serves 6

2 litres/3½ pints chicken
stock

85 g/3 oz shiitake
mushrooms, thinly sliced

175 g/6 oz pak choy or
other Oriental greens,
sliced into thin ribbons

6 spring onions, finely
sliced

salt and pepper

for the chicken balls

25 g/1 oz chicken, minced

25 g/1 oz fresh spinach
leaves, finely chopped

2 spring onions, finely
chopped

1 garlic clove, very finely
chopped

pinch of Oriental 5-spice
powder

1 tsp soy sauce

To make the chicken balls, put the chicken, spinach, spring onions and garlic in a bowl. Add the 5-spice powder and soy sauce and mix until combined.

Shape the chicken mixture into 24 balls. Place them in one layer in a steamer that will fit over the top of a saucepan.

Bring the stock just to the boil in a saucepan that will accommodate the steamer. Regulate the heat so that the liquid bubbles gently. Add the mushrooms to the stock and place the steamer, covered, on top of the pan. Steam for 10 minutes. Remove the steamer and set aside on a plate.

Add the pak choy and spring onions to the pan and cook gently in the stock for 3–4 minutes, or until the leaves are wilted. Taste the soup and adjust the seasoning, if necessary.

Divide the chicken balls evenly between warmed bowls and ladle the soup over them. Serve immediately.

bacon & ham
    bacon & lentil soup 121
    cheese & bacon soup 110
    chicken & potato soup with
        bacon 130
    split pea & ham soup 109
beans
    beef & bean soup 91
    chorizo & red kidney bean
        soup 118
    minestrone 18
    sausage & red cabbage soup 112
    tuna chowder 72
    Tuscan bean soup 32
    vegetable soup with pesto 30
beansprouts
    Asian lamb soup 100
    prawn laksa 54
    Thai chicken-coconut soup 136
beef
    beef & bean soup 91
    beef & vegetable soup 86
    beef broth with herbs &
        vegetables 97
    beef consommé with eggs &
        Parmesan 92
    chunky potato & beef soup 98
    Mexican-style beef & rice
        soup 94
    spicy beef & noodle soup 88
beef stock 9
bouillabaisse 48

cabbage
    chunky vegetable soup 17 .
    minestrone 18
    sausage & red cabbage soup 112
carrots
    chicken noodle soup 129
    chunky vegetable soup 17
    creamy carrot & parsnip soup 35
    Scotch broth 103
cheese
    beef consommé with eggs &
        Parmesan 92
    cheese & bacon soup 110
    French onion soup 23
    spinach & cheese soup 42
    sweet potato & Stilton soup 44
    turkey, leek & Stilton soup 150
chicken
    chicken & potato soup with
    chicken gumbo soup 132
    chicken, leek & prune soup 142
    chicken, mushroom & barley
        soup 141
    chicken noodle soup 129
        bacon 130
    chicken ravioli in tarragon
        broth 138
    chicken, rice & vegetable
        soup 126
    cock-a-leekie 144
    cream of chicken soup 124
    mulligatawny soup 135
    oriental chicken balls & greens in
        broth 159
    Thai chicken-coconut soup 136
chicken stock 9
chickpeas: spicy lamb soup with
        chickpeas & courgettes 104
chorizo
    chorizo & red kidney bean
        soup 118

squid, chorizo & tomato soup 68
clam & corn chowder 56
courgettes
    spicy lamb soup with chickpeas
        & courgettes 104
    vegetable soup with pesto 30
crab
    crab & vegetable soup 78
    mixed fish soup 77
cucumber
    cold cucumber & smoked salmon
        soup 62
    gazpacho 26

duck
    duck with spring onion soup 156
    oriental duck broth 154

fennel & tomato soup with
        prawns 59
fish & shellfish
    bouillabaisse 48
    Genoese fish soup 60
    mixed fish soup 77
    seafood chowder 65
    squid, chorizo & tomato soup 68
    tuna chowder 72
    see also mussels; prawns; salmon;
        scallops
fish stock 8
French onion soup 23

gazpacho 26
green beans, vegetable soup with
        pesto 30

haddock & prawn chowder 83

lamb
    Asian lamb soup 100
    lamb & rice soup 106
    Scotch broth 103
    spicy lamb soup with chickpeas
        & courgettes 104
leeks
    chicken, leek & prune soup 142
    cock-a-leekie 144
    leek & potato soup 14
    salmon & leek soup 50
    Scotch broth 103
    turkey, leek & Stilton soup 150
lentils
    bacon & lentil soup 121
    turkey & lentil soup 148
lobster bisque 71

minestrone 18
mushrooms
    chicken, mushroom & barley
        soup 141
    chunky vegetable soup 17
    creamy mushroom & tarragon
        soup 29
    duck with spring onion soup 156
    lemon turkey soup with
        mushrooms 153
    oriental chicken balls & greens in
        broth 159
    oriental duck broth 154
    turkey & lentil soup 148
    turkey soup with rice,
        mushrooms & sage 147

mussels
    bouillabaisse 48
    seafood chowder 65

noodles
    chicken noodle soup 129
    pork & vegetable broth 115
    prawn laksa 54
    spicy beef & noodle soup 88
    Thai chicken-coconut soup 136

okra: chicken gumbo soup 132
oysters: creamy oyster soup 74

parsnips: creamy carrot & parsnip
        soup 35
pasta
    chicken ravioli in tarragon
        broth 138
    minestrone 18
    Tuscan bean soup 32
pearl barley
    beef & vegetable soup 86
    chicken, mushroom & barley
        soup 141
    Scotch broth 103
peas
    chicken, rice & vegetable
        soup 126
    cream of pea soup 24
    minestrone 18
    spicy lamb soup with chickpeas
        & courgettes 104
    vegetable soup with pesto 30
peppers
    chorizo & red kidney bean
        soup 118
    crab & vegetable soup 78
    duck with spring onion soup 156
    gazpacho 26
    minestrone 18
    pork & vegetable broth 115
    pork chilli soup 117
    red pepper & orange soup 20
pork
    pork & vegetable broth 115
    pork chilli soup 117
potatoes
    cheese & bacon soup 110
    chicken & potato soup with
        bacon 130
    chorizo & red kidney bean
        soup 118
    chunky potato & beef soup 98
    chunky vegetable soup 17
    clam & corn chowder 56
    leek & potato soup 14
    sausage & red cabbage soup 112
    tuna chowder 72
    watercress soup 36
prawns
    bouillabaisse 48
    fennel & tomato soup with
        prawns 59
    Genoese fish soup 60
    haddock & prawn chowder 83
    prawn & vegetable bisque 80
    prawn laksa 54
    seafood chowder 65
    Thai-style seafood soup 53
prunes
    chicken, leek & prune soup 142
    cock-a-leekie 144

pumpkin: spiced pumpkin soup 38

rice
    chicken gumbo soup 132
    chicken, leek & prune soup 142
    chicken, rice & vegetable
        soup 126
    lamb & rice soup 106
    Mexican-style beef & rice
        soup 94
    mulligatawny soup 135
    turkey soup with rice,
        mushrooms & sage 147

salmon
    cold cucumber & smoked salmon
        soup 62
    salmon & leek soup 50
sausage & red cabbage soup 112
scallops
    bouillabaisse 48
    seared scallops in garlic broth 66
    Thai-style seafood soup 53
Scotch broth 103
spinach
    spinach & cheese soup 42
    vegetable soup with pesto 30
squash: roasted squash, sweet
        potato & garlic soup 41
squid, chorizo & tomato soup 68
stocks 8–9
sweetcorn
    chunky potato & beef soup 98
    chunky vegetable soup 17
    clam & corn chowder 56
    crab & vegetable soup 78
    haddock & prawn chowder 83
    mixed fish soup 77
sweet potatoes
    roasted squash, sweet potato &
        garlic soup 41
    sweet potato & Stilton soup 44

tomatoes
    Asian lamb soup 100
    beef & bean soup 91
    bouillabaisse 48
    chicken gumbo soup 132
    chunky vegetable soup 17
    fennel & tomato soup with
        prawns 59
    gazpacho 26
    Genoese fish soup 60
    Mexican-style beef & rice
        soup 94
    minestrone 18
    pork chilli soup 117
    spicy lamb soup with chickpeas
        & courgettes 104
    squid, chorizo & tomato soup 68
    tomato soup 12
    tuna chowder 72
    turkey & lentil soup 148
tuna chowder 72
turkey
    lemon turkey soup with
        mushrooms 153
    turkey & lentil soup 148
    turkey, leek & Stilton soup 150
    turkey soup with rice,
        mushrooms & sage 147

vegetable stock 8

watercress soup 36